The Principal's Cycle

A Blueprint for the Inexperienced and Experienced Principal

The Principal's Cycle

A Blueprint for the Inexperienced and Experienced Principal

Keith T. Stephenson, Ed.D

Foreword by Randolph Mitchell, Ph.D.

Edited by Sara Burns

The Principal's Cycle

ISBN 978-0-578-08741-2

Dedicated to Bryce, Justin, and Grant
Through your veins flow wisdom, power, and understanding.

It is wise to keep in mind that
neither success nor failure is ever final.

~Roger Babson

"With the continued advances in electronic media, our email boxes are often filled with notifications of the latest publications that purport to tell educators how to succeed. Unfortunately, most are written by individuals long removed from the schoolhouse. Keith Stephenson's book, *The Principal's Cycle*, represents a meaningful and practical guide that will help a new principal get started on the right track, or help seasoned administrators reposition themselves for a more successful school year. Keith is a successful principal who "walks the walk." I am proud to have him on my team!"

Donald L. Hense
Founder and Chairman
Friendship Public Charter School

Contents

Forward by Randolph Mitchell, Ph.D. 1

Preface 3

1. Overview of the Principalship 5

2. July 17

3. August 25

4. September 39

5. October 47

6. November 53

7. December 59

8. January 65

9. February - March 69

10. April - May 75

11. June 81

Conclusion 85

Appendix 87

Forward
by Randolph Mitchell, Ph.D.

At a time when educators are in a vigorous search for plausible solutions to many of the common problems that are plaguing the nation's schools, Keith Stephenson's observations in this book are timely. The Principal's Cycle is a brilliant step-by-step guide that creates a clear picture for new and seasoned principals alike. It is insightful and practical, and it tackles the everyday issues, problems, and concerns that principals confront as they journey through the world of instructional leadership.

Dr. Stephenson deals with specific issues that, if not handled appropriately, can lead to a serious lack of productivity and ultimately the failure of the school. As an urban school leader, he is well aware that the key ingredient to a student's success is attention to detail. It is clear that his knowledge, education, and experiences have provided him the ability (sometimes unique) to identify the common pitfalls that result in the failure of inexperienced principals. His systematic approach to leading schools has greatly contributed to the productivity of the schools he was charged to lead. Since the advent of NCLB, we have not only seen a great deal of emphasis placed on instruction, but also a significant amount of emphasis placed on the many activities that support effective education. Through his writing, Dr. Stephenson deals with all aspects of the instructional process as seen and managed by the principal. He covers the spectrum from classroom instruction during the school year through the importance of planning during traditional down times and summer months. The simplicity and ease with which Dr. Stephenson navigates his readers through the bends and turns of the daily, monthly, and quarterly trials, tribulations, and triumphs of the schoolhouse is brilliant! Rarely does an exposé on the principalship ever detail the encounters of the job in such vivid detail. His knowledge and experience lend themselves to the adept solutions he proposes for the variety of leadership challenges principals face.

This concise, succinct dialogue is rich with anecdotal examples of the typical occurrences encountered in the school setting. His contribution to the body of knowledge of schooling serves as a reference to anyone thinking of pursuing the challenge of educational leadership. It is evident that Dr. Stephenson understands the balance between ensuring that all details in a school are covered and making certain that the concepts of high expectations are instilled in his staff. He intimates the importance of all factors (big and small) central to the success in overseeing the educational process. Throughout the book, he explores the importance of not only keeping staff involved in the decision making process, but instilling a sense of responsibility for having them accept this role. Dr. Stephenson offers systematic approaches for achieving this goal.

In education we know that students often rise to the expectations set by their teachers. Throughout the book, Dr. Stephenson repeatedly emphasizes the importance of effectively planning and establishing high expectations to serve as the foundation of a school. The Principal's Cycle is a necessity for all educators who are interested in pursuing or currently serving in an administrative role.

Preface

Throughout this book, for the sake of brevity, I refer to principals in the male gender, though some of the best principals I know are women. So, let it be known to one and all, my grammatical expediency is not meant to overlook nor neglect the contributions made by our female counterparts.

CHAPTER 1

Overview of the Principalship

In schools, the principal plays the most critical role. Its importance can only be compared to the point guard on a basketball team or a quarterback on a football team. Like a point guard or quarterback of a team failing to effectively perform, a substandard principal will inevitably result in the demise of a school.

In the current age of education, the No Child Left Behind act has added to the pressures associated with the role of the principal. Even though principals have a wide array of responsibilities they must fulfill, student achievement is the primary focus of the school. Student achievement is published annually for the community to view. Schools failing to achieve academically can possibly lose their principals and staff members. With such incredibly high stakes, it is critical for principals to gain a comprehensive picture of an entire school year. The sooner this occurs, the higher the trajectory of the school leader.

The goal of this book is to provide new principals with a guide that will result in success in all areas of the principalship within one year. Over time, the school year becomes a very cyclical process for the principal. Unfortunately, the pace for a first- year principal is unfathomable. Those who fail to adjust to this blazing pace will most likely resign or be terminated. To provide new principals with a manuscript to use as a guide during their entire first year, this book will be organized by each month. In addition, the book will provide principals with additional tips to strengthen their chances of being successful.

Instructional Leader versus Manager

In the last ten years, the term instructional leader has often been used to label the role of the principal. Whether instructional leader is the most current buzzword or instruction is the primary focus of the principal, the role of the principal is comprised of a multitude of tasks and responsibilities that extend well beyond instructional leadership. While the effectiveness of a principal can often be linked directly to annual testing scores, test scores are only one indicator of the success of a school. Can a principal be effective if his school is perceived as an unsafe environment? Can a principal be considered effective if he has repeatedly failed to balance the school budget? If these conditions characterize your school, should test scores/instruction remain your focal point as the principal?

The principalship requires a vast amount of leadership skills, aside from instruction. High quality instruction can only occur if a principal is a proficient manager first. While the principal can not be an expert in all areas of a school, he will be forced to make decisions in a variety of areas including staff attendance, facilities, custodial requirements, budget, athletics, bomb threats, etc., all having nothing to do with the teaching and learning process. A principal needs to possess a basic understanding of all aspects of a school. Great principals gain the respect and credibility of all staff members within a school, regardless of their role.

Successful principals are able to balance all the responsibilities of managing a school and still maintain a focus on the instructional program. To achieve this focus, issues aside from instruction must be handled in an expedient fashion. Failure to make decisions quickly will result in the principal being bogged down with issues not related to the focal point of the school. While this balance is difficult to achieve, it plays a critical role in the success of a principal.

Demands of the Job

Simply put, the principalship is a job that never ends. Unlike the majority of staff members who work ten months, the principal works 12 months per year. Contrary to popular beliefs, principals often work their hardest during the summer months. Due to the extensive planning and staff hiring required to successfully open schools in August/September, principals often work long hours during the summer months.

During the school year, the amount of time required to do an outstanding job varies. During the week, there will definitely be times when the principal must work late. For example, evening concerts, open house events, and select PTA meetings are events that require an administrative presence. If the school does not have assistant principals, then attendance at these events is the responsibility of the principal. Aside from the public appearances that are required, the daily workload of the principal can be overwhelming.

From responding to dozens of emails on a daily basis to completing teacher evaluations, the job is filled with tasks that must be completed. In addition, principals spend an inordinate part of the school day visiting classrooms, meeting with parents, and attending meetings. Therefore, the principal can only tackle his work after students and teachers are dismissed from school. The workload of the principal is never completed; it can only be controlled by the amount of effort and skill level demonstrated by the principal.

Rest and Recovery

The principalship, like many other leadership positions, will result in stressful days and sleepless nights. To combat the stress associated with the job, it is critical that you find ways to rejuvenate both your mind and body. People achieve this in a variety of ways. I always maintained an active social life that did not include staff members. In addition, I remained focused on working with my wife to raise our children.

Regardless of how you decide to rest and recover, it is important to commit the time to doing so. Burnout is a reality that can be avoided if you take the appropriate steps.

As a principal, I would not work during single-day holidays (e.g. Labor Day). With approximately 10 days of holidays per year, this helped to maintain a balance. During extended holidays (e.g. Winter Break, Spring Break), I limited the number of hours I worked. For example, if the school allowed 10 days for Winter Break, I would generally work half days or take at least 3-4 days off. For half days, I would get to the office around 10:00 a.m., go to lunch around 12:30 p.m., report back to work around 1:45 p.m., and leave around 3:30. If you adopt this schedule, you will be able to complete your necessary tasks without the burden of working an entire day. More importantly, it will provide you an opportunity to regroup and revitalize yourself without using entire days of leave.

The Principal as a Public Relations Person

If left alone, a school will take on an entire life of its own. The principal has a responsibility to serve as an excellent public relations person for the school. In the best interests of the school, the principal needs to assemble the school staff to set expectations regarding how it should be perceived by the public. Just like bad public relations can consume a school community, good public relations can have a positive impact on the larger school community. While every school has its problems, all problems do not need to be public information. The principal possesses the power to dictate the tone as it relates to public relations.

In the world of No Child Left Behind, a picture of the school is often generated based solely on academic and attendance data. While these data points are surely important, a school is much more than an academic record as it relates to a standardized test. In virtually all schools, great things are happening that often go unnoticed. The principal and staff have a responsibility to highlight those things. They can include honor roll names, field trips, the names of volunteers, student citizenship, etc. A monthly newsletter and calendar would be an excellent way to highlight events that support your academic program within a school. Parents like to hear positive things about their child's school, so school staff has a responsibility to promote these types of events. The principal is the driving force behind the public relations machine.

You are the Exemplar

As much as a principal may try to deny it, every person associated with the school looks for guidance from the principal. With this in mind, it is critical that principals understand the importance of the role they play in school communities. Principals should set the standard within a school. For example, principals cannot hold teachers accountable for being punctual for work if the principal is consistently late for work. The actions of principals are evaluated and re-evaluated to not only scrutinize the decision, but also to determine the standard and precedence being established.

All principals possess unique leadership styles. Each principal will have to determine his own leadership style to lead a school. With principals tailoring schools to serve the diverse needs of students, parents, and teachers, each principal requires a specific skill set to be successful. As a new principal, the way in which you adjust to your individual situation will be scrutinized. The figurative microscope will be used by all the various stakeholders, not just a few. Effective principals understand the power they possess as leaders and use it to their advantage. They understand the importance of modeling a high work ethic for their staff. By behaving in a manner that you expect staff to follow, principals shape the overall culture of a school.

Evolutionary vs. Revolutionary Leadership

As with any leadership position, the principalship requires one to lead through a variety of situations. Evolutionary and revolutionary leadership styles are at opposite ends of a continuum. As the concept relates to schools, a principal who is building the capacity to sustain long-term growth characterizes evolutionary leadership. The plan for long-term growth includes the staff that is currently working in the school. At the other end of the spectrum is revolutionary leadership. This form of leadership is characterized by a principal who is also striving for growth and progress; however, the long-term plan does not include current staff. The current staff members are likely to be transferred or terminated from their positions. Revolutionary leadership may require decisions that lead to instant changes or "shaking things up." While both leadership styles have the goal of long-term growth, the two styles are fundamentally different by their means of achieving their goals.

As a principal, you must be able to utilize both leadership styles. There will be instances when an entire staff is forced to reapply for their jobs and the principal must make the "revolutionary" decision. The final decision is always difficult; however, revolutionary decision should only be made for the sake of evolutionary progress. For example, terminating an inadequate social studies teacher should only be executed if the replacement is likely to bring stability and potential to the position. Thoughtless evolutionary leadership decisions may contribute to the lack of trust within an organization and be perceived as reckless leadership.

Managing the Workload

Student recommendation letters, teacher evaluations, emails, parent meetings, focus walks, and administrative meetings are just the start of your responsibilities as they relate to your principalship. If you love to work, the principalship is the perfect job. There will be recurring issues that keep you working late into the evenings and awake at night. The key to managing your never-ending workload is to create healthy work routines. Each principal works differently. As a principal, I tended to end my workday between 6:00 and 6:30 p.m. Also, I liked to work for two to three hours on Sunday nights. That provided excellent insight into the oncoming week and allowed me to focus my week's work. In speaking with my colleagues, some preferred to start their workday one to two hours before staff arrived, giving them a head start each day. Other principals worked one or two late nights, 8:30-9:00, per week. Regardless how you plan to do it, just know that the workload never lets up. As the principal, you will need to find a way to manage the volume of work.

One solution is to create and follow systems. Who checks your emails? Do you set your own calendar? Can parents meet with you at any time of the day? As the principal, should you conduct personal interviews of students transferring to the school in the middle of the year? All of the aforementioned questions can be part of a system. For example, due to the high volume of emails received during a typical school day (as high as 40), I felt that I needed an email screener to determine the importance of each email. Upon starting my principalship, I discovered that all email senders mark their emails as important. From the principal's perspective, only 20%-30% of daily emails are actually important. Because of the high percentage of "junk" emails, I was wasting too much time sorting through pointless advertisements and sales pitches. Currently, my secretary screens my emails and labels the legitimate ones in red. This system has been very effective in my quest to save time.

As previously stated, solid routines support your efforts in becoming a proficient principal. Routines like conducting classroom visits in the morning, providing regular instructional feedback to teachers, and celebrating the success of staff can support your growth. All too often, the workload and pressure to perform can result in the principal spending countless hours in his office. Each day, I recommend that the principal start by walking around the school, not sitting in the office. Depending on the size of the school, you may need to visit certain parts of the building on certain days. Most importantly, do not start the day (once children arrive) near your office. I even found that being located on floors/wings away from the main office led to more productive times. Since parents tend to escort younger students into the school, the first floor was always a trap. In my mind, parents do not understand the complexity of the principalship. Depending on the demeanor of the principal, parents feel free to talk for extended periods , regardless of the current mission of the principal. Healthy routines minimize time loss.

One of the mistakes that many principals make is the underutilization of their secretaries. Aside from the assistant principal, the secretary is the most important administrative position on the staff and must possess the appropriate character traits. The root word of secretary is secret. Due to the amount of confidential information that the secretary is exposed to, he or she must be able to keep a secret. Information leaks from the secretary can damage the work of the principal. I encourage principals to carefully assess the use of their secretaries. Upon their entry into school, the secretary handles mail, telephone calls, staff members, and parents. The secretary must create a welcoming environment for all. In all situations, including the expectation established by the principal, the secretary must always behave in a professional manner. Due to the scattered nature of their job, they must be proficient at multi-tasking. As previously stated, they serve as the first line of public relations for the school. Principals can use secretaries to complete other tasks as well, including sending mail, responding to emails, directing incoming calls to the appropriate people, maintaining the principal's schedule, making monthly calendars, updating the marquee, distributing package deliveries, and making announcements. This is just a short list that was specific to schools where I worked-- your school will require a unique set of secretarial needs. As the principal, determine how best you can utilize your secretary. Failure to do so will result in inefficiency and will add to your hours at work.

Principals despise meetings. Upon accepting your new principalship, you will feel as if you are meeting all the time. As the leader of the school, you must understand the rationale behind your meetings and use them to your advantage. Contrary to popular belief, meetings are important. They allow you to control the direction of the school by communicating with your staff. To maximize their effectiveness, you should consider the following: Schedule regular meetings with teams/committees. This promotes consistency in discussions and provides the principal an opportunity to assess the status of the team on an ongoing basis. Create agendas for meetings and distribute them at least one day before the meeting. Effective agendas bring focus to meetings. Distributing agendas beforehand allows the participants to prepare for agenda items that will be discussed. This results in richer conversations that support better meetings. As a part of your agenda, include time estimates for each agenda item. Start and end meetings in a timely fashion. As a principal, you will have multiple meetings to attend each day. You are often the one person from your school who will attend all these meetings. Other participants do not have much interest in the fact that the meeting at 11:00 a.m. is the principal's third meeting of the day. Hypothetically, if each meeting ran over by 15 minutes, the 11:00 a.m. meeting started 30 minutes late. Regardless of the type of meeting, the participants' time should be respected. As a school leader, I had a five-minute rule; all meetings must start and finish within five minutes of the pre-determined time. For principals, meetings are a necessary evil. Use them to articulate and re-emphasize your vision of the school.

As a new principal, you will be amazed by the amount of information you are expected to remember. From teacher requests to student investigations, people expect the principal to remember all the details of your conversation. Due to the nature of the principalship, it is possible that conversations held in the morning are simply not remembered by the evening. Even though as a principal you tend to be a sharp thinker, do not rely solely on your memory. Furthermore, because you may need this information in the future, it is best to keep it in a notebook. I recommend a notebook as opposed to loose sheets of paper. Notebooks allow you to keep information in an organized fashion. I divide the information into four sections: teacher/staff information, student information, parent information, and miscellaneous information. Since 95% of the information that I receive can be classified in the four major sections, I always have a record of the various discussions. This allows me to access information in an expeditious fashion for years to come.

There is a saying--peace cannot be achieved without war. This is not only true with world powers, but also schools. As the principal, you must find a way to hold your staff members accountable without burning out. The challenge with holding everyone accountable is that there are only 24 hours in a day. Many inexperienced principals make the mistake of writing long letters to staff members who violate school policies. While documenting staff behaviors is important, letters are not always needed. Imagine that you have 20 of your 25 teachers who are not retrieving their students in a timely manner from elective (e.g., music, art, physical education, foreign language)classes. Do you write 20 letters of reprimand to these teachers? As a seasoned principal, I feel that writing actual letters for such minor violations is a waste of time. While I agree these behaviors need to be addressed, a simple checklist could serve as documentation to curb undesired behaviors. Using a checklist allows you to document the behaviors of your entire staff in 15 minutes. Reserve the letter writing campaigns for serious violations. Feel free to reference these checklists during mid-year and annual evaluation conferences. Staff members comply with directives and expectations when they realize their behaviors are being documented.

The last tip for managing your workload is based on a lesson that I learned the hard way. Like the information overload that you will experience, you will also experience date overload. As a principal, you will have obligations that pull you from the building on a regular basis. Do not rely on your memory--it will definitely fail you. You must create a calendar system to keep your dates. Whether you use an Internet calendar, "Outlook", or paper datebook, you will definitely need a method to organize your events, meetings, conferences, etc. You don't want to miss an important meeting because of poor organization.

CHAPTER 2

July

Chapter 2 includes the following subjects:
- The importance of understanding why you were hired
- Staff Politics
- Effective Starting Points
- Focal Points
- July Goals

W hile most school systems have identified principals long before July, the end of June is a common start date for new principals. Even though the start of school seems like a long time away, the summer months pass very quickly. Furthermore, summer is the time when most of the district employees take vacation leave, making it difficult to complete tasks in an efficient manner. Principals need to have a firm plan for the summer months. Failure to create a daily, weekly, and monthly plan may serve as the downfall for a principal in a new school. An effective plan should include staffing goals, opening-of-school plans, emergency evacuation plans, weekly staff tasks, teacher/student letters, etc. The more that a new principal plans, the more prepared he will be. Planning is the key.

In planning for the year, the incoming principal needs to gain a clear understanding of the reason behind his hiring. A principal who is hired to transform a failing school will probably have a different plan than the principal who inherited a high-performing school. A summer plan is critical for each school; however, the goal of each plan will be significantly different. Identifying the reason behind your hiring can serve as a foundation for your summer plan.

After determining the reason for your hiring, it is critical to identify the key people within the school. Often known as "power brokers," they will help with the initial planning process and early initiatives. Even though these people will be more than willing to provide support, one must be aware of possible ulterior motives. The power brokers will have insight into the inner workings of the staff that the incoming principal will fail to have. For example, during these planning sessions, suggestions regarding teacher and room assignments could be made. Unbeknownst to the principal, these issues may have served as a point of contention with the outgoing principal. As a result, the incoming principal is introduced to issues from the outset. Staff personalities will play a critical role in pushing the agenda of the principal. Step lightly at first, but more importantly, try to determine the power brokers as soon as possible.

Where Should I Start?

After a principal is selected to lead a school, there is not much time to waste if the plan is to open school in a timely and orderly fashion. With principalships beginning in July, the turnaround for August/September is less than six weeks away. Several things, both internally and externally, must be completed in an expeditious fashion.

When accepting the position, you must understand what type of leadership skills you will need to improve the school. With this knowledge, it is critical that you hire administrators who will complement your leadership style. With larger schools that require numerous assistant principals, it may be necessary to diversify the gender of your administrators. When dealing with both male and female students, having male and female administrators will be beneficial in working through gender-specific issues. In addition to gender diversity, creating an administrative team that is racially reflective of the student body may support your efforts with winning over parents and students.

Once your administrative team is in place, you will need to gain an understanding of the needs of the entire school, including students, staff, and parents. A comprehensive assessment of the school will need to be conducted as soon as possible. To complicate matters, this assessment will be conducted during the summer months, when school is not in session. This assessment will drive your early work as the principal.

Many new principals may ask the question "How do principals conduct an assessment of the school without staff and students being present?" Based on NCLB labels, a school would already know its "report card"; however, there are many indicators that provide insight into a school. Promotion rates, report card grades, suspension rates, teacher attendance, truancy rates, master schedule, elective schedules, and teacher retention rates all help to create a picture of the school. In addition, informal and formal parent meetings throughout the summer can provide useful feedback regarding how the larger community perceives the school. Even though the feedback from parents and staff is helpful, the principal must still be aware of the stakeholders who attempt to further their own agendas by providing misguided feedback.

After gaining an understanding of the needs of the school, the principal must know the specifics of the facility. While custodians will be most familiar with the facility, the principal should also have a clear understanding of the layout of the building. It is critical in planning logistical procedures including fire drills, entry/dismissal routines, shelter-in-place procedures, etc. Because the principal is responsible for designing and executing these plans when necessary, it is critical to have a working knowledge of the school building.

Focal Points

An organizational culture exists in any organization. As the principal, your work helps to shape and define that culture. Compared to the actual school year, the summer tends to support a more relaxed environment. While the summer tempo is a bit slower than that of the fall, a tremendous amount of planning must be completed during the summer months. The principal must establish a tone of seriousness as it relates to summer work. You will be amazed at how little will be achieved if the summer staff is not serious about completing tasks.

Even though the principal must be the mastermind behind summer planning, the expertise of the staff must be utilized. The summer staff is often referred to as "12-month" employees. Summer staff sometimes include secretaries, special education coordinators, guidance counselors, custodians, and security guards. While their roles are clearly defined during the school year, the relaxed mood, coupled with the lack of structure that exists during the rest of the year, may naturally result in a lack of productivity.

To address this substandard work ethic, the principal must lead by example. More important than holding summer staff accountable, the principal must adhere to work hours and deadlines. Regular staff meetings to assess summer progress are a necessity. Like regular school staff, summer staff will also be watching the actions of the principal. If the principal fails to meet the mark, summer staff will also fall short. Simply put, the principal's action will set the tone within the school.

Many principals, in their newly-appointed posts, fail to have a strategic plan. The creation of a plan, organized by week, provides direction and establishes a standard for summer work. The plan must include specific tasks and a person who is responsible for completing each task. The plan could include tasks such as staffing, resetting locker combinations, sending welcome letters to staff, inventory of textbooks, creating staff mailboxes, and completing scheduling. Admittedly, the aforementioned list is scant; however, due to the unique nature of each school, your list will differ significantly. Your strategic plan should include all tasks needed for a successful opening of school. Weekly meetings should be held to assess progress and discuss any modifications to the plan.

July Goals

July is a critical month. In most instances, if mistakes are discovered in July, they can be resolved by the start of the school year. There are a number of critical areas that must be comprehensively assessed in July. The understanding of staffing, facility, master schedule, supplies, and textbooks must be obtained as early as possible.

Staffing, master schedule, and student enrollment needs are all dependent on each other. Instructional staff must be aligned with the master schedule, and that schedule must be designed to address the instructional needs of all students who are enrolled at the school. For example, if the total number of third grade students requires five third-grade sections, then you must staff for five teachers. In turn, the master schedule must make accommodations for five third-grade sections. Lunches, teachers' planning periods, and special classes (i.e., art, music, PE), as they relate to the master schedule, are driven by the number of sections and school enrollment. Based on this specific scenario, if you plan on having common planning periods for each grade level, you will need five electives teachers to relieve your third-grade teachers for their planning period. Master schedule decisions should be made early to ensure ample time to hire staff before the start of school.

In the previous chapter, I discussed the importance of understanding the facility and I emphasize it further here. Due to the long hours that you will inevitably spend at work, the school will serve as your palace. From classroom assignments to evacuation plans, you will need to gain a comprehensive understanding of the school, inclusive of the school grounds, within your first weeks on the job. Your responsibility of assigning every inch of the building to a staff member is critical and should not be done with a vague understanding of the facility. This list, as limited as it may be, will provide insight into the thought process related to the school facility. Locker assignments, fire drill routes, supply storage, computer storage, bulletin board assignments, bell system, stairwells, restrooms, hidden nooks and crannies, exterior doorways, access to rooftops, playgrounds, exterior walkways, exterior steps, hazardous walkways, and parking lots are all things that you need to be fully aware of by mid July. One may ask, "Why do I need to know the path that cars take to enter the parking lot?" If breakfast for students begins at 8:00 a.m. and teachers are due to arrive at the same time, the principal needs to ensure that cars do not serve as a hazard for students. An accident attributed to the lack of planning is very difficult for a principal to justify.

Another area that needs to be assessed by mid-July is storage, specifically the storage of expensive equipment such as televisions, computers, printers, DVD players, etc. Items that are not only used in schools, but also used at home are hot commodities for theft. Overhead projectors do not really have a "street value"; therefore, they tend to remain in schools. Flat screen televisions are light and can be sold relatively easily. With this said, shortly after your arrival, take an inventory of the storage area that houses expensive items. I would also recommend changing the lock on the storage closet. Since you will be new to the building, you will have no idea who possesses the keys to various locations throughout the building. The transitional time between two principals is perceived as an opportunity for opportunists.

Along with your new position of principal comes your responsibility to introduce yourself to students, parents, and staff members. The easiest way to reach all of these stakeholders is to craft a welcome letter. The welcome letter to students/parents should include the vision of your instructional program, various course offerings, a list of extra-curricular activities, and any major changes that have occurred over the summer. The letter should be optimistic in its mood and provide the audience with something to look forward to. Remember, this letter will probably serve as your first introduction to your students and parents, so make sure to represent yourself and the new position well.

Even though you are the new principal of the school, it is highly possible that you know only a few staff members so far. Depending on the interview or selection process, you may not know any staff members. When this is the case, staff members try to get an idea about their new boss by asking teachers of your former school or others who may know you. The welcome letter that you provide may be the first official document generated by their new leader. Like the previous welcome letter, it should be positive in mood. You may want to include your instructional vision and steps that you have taken to ensure a smooth opening of school. Historically, if vacancies have been an issue, you may want to include information regarding your staffing. Please refrain from including major changes that are on the horizon. This may be incorrectly perceived as the new principal making premature wholesale changes. Undoubtedly, staff members will scrutinize the initial welcome letter for hidden meanings. Make the letter work for you.

The summer is a busy time of year for the delivery of supplies. Unfortunately, if not managed appropriately, supplies will quickly disappear over the summer months. The person responsible for managing the acceptance of supplies must account for everything that is delivered. In addition, these supplies must remain in a secure location. Since the teachers who ordered the supplies the previous March/April will not be present until August, there is a period of at least one month when things can disappear or end up in other teachers' classrooms. Like the electronic equipment, this transition time between leaders serves as an opportunity for people to seize materials that they have not ordered.

New principals should take inventory of the supplies that they will need to successfully open the school year. If this is done in July, there is ample time for the delivery of new materials before the start of school. These materials include, but are certainly not limited to, paper, pencils, journals, textbooks, notebooks, bulletin board paper, etc. Failure to provide the basic necessities to teachers may be perceived as an inadequate plan by the principal. Assess as soon as possible and order new supplies promptly. July allows enough time for problems to be resolved before the start of school.

Considering all the tasks that need to be completed in July, it is clear that it is a critical month. The best part about July is that you still have time to correct existing errors before the start of school. Effective work in July puts you in striking range of an outstanding opening of the school year. Take advantage of July.

* * * * *

SCENARIO

As I entered my office on my official start date, my mind raced with all the tasks that I needed to complete before the start of school. In my first hour on the job, parents were requesting to speak with the new principal, students were anxious to meet the new leader, and teachers were eager to learn what they could about their new boss. The juggling act begins immediately. In moving forward, how do you keep all stakeholders satisfied and still satisfy all of the demands of the job? As a new principal, that will be the key to your success. Just remember, all stakeholders are important; however, students are your most important stakeholders. If you make decisions in the best interests of students, you will rarely make the wrong decision.

Questions to Consider:

- How will you prioritize your decisions that have an actual impact on students' academic and social performance?
- How do you courteously dismiss individuals who are trying to achieve their personal agenda?
- What is your plan to manage all the tasks that need to be completed?

CHAPTER 3

August

Chapter 3 includes the following subjects :
- Organizing the School
- Planning the First Day
- Creating Healthy Routines and Rituals
- Planning the First Day for Staff Members
- Identifying School-Based Leadership

D epending on the date of the first day of school, the pressure will begin to build during the month of August. Schools located in northern states generally start after Labor Day; schools located in the south generally begin in late August. In either case, August will serve as the month when the majority of your logistical planning will occur.

After having the month of July to gain an understanding of staff needs and the facility, August is the perfect time to assign classrooms to teachers, offices to staff members, and storage areas to departments. On face value, this does not appear to be a major task; however, the placement of staff within the school plays a major role in creating a healthy school culture. In the next few paragraphs, I will provide thinking points around staff placement.

As the new principal of the school, one of the major decisions you will need to make is the assignment of teachers to classrooms. Since every principal has his own approach to assigning classrooms, it will be virtually impossible for every teacher to remain in last year's classroom. Before assigning classrooms, consider the needs of your school. If you have a school where grade levels are departmentalized, resulting in students having to move from class to class, you must consider this. In this case, I recommend that you assign the teachers who teach common students in classrooms near each other. This minimizes class change times and maximizes teacher supervision of students. In cases where this cannot happen due to facility constraints, classroom assignments should still be a thoughtful process. For example, if science laboratories are all housed in the east wing of the building, try to resist the temptation to assign additional subjects to that area. You may want to label the east wing as your science wing. This would limit the number of students who enter the east wing only to those who have science.

For elementary schools, I recommend that common grade levels be assigned to classrooms in close proximity. This encourages teacher collaboration and supports team teaching. Whenever possible, I would assign your teachers who are strong classroom managers to rooms near the main office or conference rooms. If a parent is in the office to discuss his child's behavior issues, you do not want a chaotic classroom right across the hall. This situation works against the principal for the entire meeting.

Specials classes must be assigned with care. For example, music, choir, or physical education classes should not be placed next to "regular" classrooms. Due to the nature of their classrooms, where students are expected to be active, this can serve as a major disturbance to other classes. You may not want to have these classrooms located near the main office. These classes frequently require more transitions with students entering and leaving. As a result, visitors always observe students in the hallway. Visitors may perceive this as chaotic student activity.

Offices must also be selected in a thoughtful manner. Since students will be expected to travel to offices, including the guidance counselor, nurse suite, social workers, etc., it is important to place these offices in accessible areas, but away from main thoroughfares, whenever possible. Students often seek the support from staff assigned to these offices during times of crisis. Again, the average onlooker will perceive the school as out of control. I know the perfect placement of these offices is difficult; however, a variety of factors must be taken into account when assigning offices.

Classroom and office assignments do not appear to be a major task but the possessive nature of people can complicate matters. Teachers are not overly willing to give up what they perceive to be their space, especially when asking them to move to a smaller classroom. An approach to make this request a bit easier is to have teachers store their belongings in common storage areas at the conclusion of the school year. Since no teachers' belongings are in a particular classroom, this eliminates the feeling of entitlement as it relates to a specific classroom. As a new principal, know that your actions throughout this process will be scrutinized, especially by veteran staff who are asked to sacrifice their room for something less inviting.

Storage is a very important component to a school. The importance of storage is easily overlooked unless you fail to have enough. Even in the most spacious schools, storage will probably be limited. As the principal, you must understand the importance of maximizing storage spaces. While the principal will probably delegate the management of storage areas to another staff member, he must have a general idea as to where supplies are kept. I recommend that storage areas be cleaned at least once per year. A good time to clean storage rooms is after supplies are distributed and school is in session. This minimizes the possibility of discarding items that teachers will need. Since teachers have an idea of what they will need throughout the year, I would suggest that teams of teachers work to maintain their own storage areas. Although storage areas appear to be harmless, fire officials often cite them for being hazardous. If the violations are not handled during the school year, the principal will be responsible for addressing the violations during the summer months, when '10-month" employees are nowhere to be found. Understanding your storage needs in August will contribute to the smooth opening of school.

After the master schedule is completed, staff hired, and facility understood, the principal needs to begin to visualize how a typical day will look. It is important to design the operation of your school. Consideration should be given to the following: How will class transitions occur or will all students use the same door to enter the school? What type of hall pass system are you planning to use? How are students expected to get from their classroom to the nurse's suite? How are disciplinary actions handled during the middle of the day? Even though this is a brief list, many things must be considered when you think of the typical day. They need to be understood and implemented when your staff returns in August. As the principal, you must be able to articulate the details of the operational plan to your staff. I recommend that you gather the staff upon their return and take them step-by-step through a typical day. When you are finished, encourage the staff to ask questions regarding the handling of normal events throughout a typical school day. This will help everyone to visualize their effectiveness.

Welcome Back Staff Meeting

Whether your staff returns to school in August or September, the Welcome Back staff meeting needs to be thoroughly planned. As the new principal, your staff will develop opinions about you based on this meeting. In most cases, this will be your first opportunity to speak will your entire staff at one time. Depending on the reason for your hiring, as discussed in Chapter 1, you will need to plan this meeting strategically. Because the staff will have an actual understanding of the school, and the principal will have an understanding simply based on hearsay, the principal is at a disadvantage. Sometimes, new principals make the mistake of forcing their agenda on teachers before they really understand the finer points of the organization. Even if you were hired to be the revolutionary leader, you still need to be strategic in your plan. There are many ways to plan your first staff meeting to create an inclusive, welcoming feeling and minimize the attention on the principal. Having staff present different segments of the meeting works very well. In addition, having staff work in cooperative groups and present their findings is also a great idea.

For the principal, the key to the first staff meeting is to gain an understanding of the staff and demonstrate competence. To avoid the "here comes another change" mindset that staff often possesses when new leadership is installed, focus on your day-to-day plan. Focus on the framework of staff responsibilities, expectations, and standards. Since you were not previously present in the school, avoid negative references to last year. This may be very difficult, especially in schools with heavily data-driven cultures. Even in these instances, do not draw conclusions about staff based on data alone. Just remember, you will have first hand experience with the staff in less than a week. At that point, you will be in a position to know exactly where the problems lie. Moving forward, your short-term plan to lead the school is critical. Share your systems and procedures for leading the school. Do not discuss things that you have little or no knowledge about. Succeeding in this initial staff meeting is crucial. Be strategic in its plan.

One of the more difficult tasks that you will be charged with is identifying school-based leadership. Under ordinary circumstances, this is not a problem; however, without having worked with building level personnel, appointing leaders is significantly more difficult. The first issue--your predecessor may have appointed team leaders and department chairpersons before leaving. Refusing them the opportunity to lead may be more trouble than it is worth. Since the new principal will have very little insight into who is capable of excelling in a leadership role, it may be easier to go with your predecessor's recommendations, at least early on. I would recommend creating leadership positions for half-year terms. Terms of half year will allow you to observe leaders at work. In August, announce that the term of the leadership positions will be for the first half of the year. In January, this will allow you to make an informed decision about leadership roles in the future. This scenario is a win-win for both teachers and the principal.

As a new principal, it is critical that you conduct a student/parent orientation before the students' first day of school. As you know, orientations can have various formats. Some principals design their orientations with students participating in a mock school day, while others consist of a meeting. Either way, the orientation should include a general overview, highlighting any major changes that will be new to the school year. If given the chance, you may also want to provide parents with their child's new classroom assignments. This will enable you to address parents' concerns related to class assignments before the first day of school. A "meet and greet" or "chew and chat" is a great way to conclude an orientation. It provides an opportunity for students and parents to meet with staff members and teachers in a non-threatening environment.

Your final task before school starts is to plan the entire first week of school. Indeed, the first week of school is a planned event. Many things need to occur during the first week including distributing lockers, textbooks, forms that need to be signed, supply lists, and student schedules (just to name a few). All of these events need to be coordinated. Failure to pay attention to the details will result in a chaotic start to the school year. Tasks like locker and textbook distributions may require modifications to the daily schedule. So teachers can plan their lessons accordingly, they appreciate early notice regarding schedule changes. As with most responsibilities related to leading a school, effective planning is critical in the operation of the school.

The First Day of School

One can argue that the first day of school is the most important day of the school year. I agree that it is important, but in reality, it is one of approximately 180 days of a school year. Day one is extremely critical and can set a tone that makes success attainable early in the school year. Day one will only be a success if the principal prepares for it appropriately. Preparation for day one must begin as early as possible. Due to the unique needs of each school and school system, day one looks different from school to school.

Let's consider some of the factors that you must account for when planning for day one. Some schools require parents to register/withdraw students upon their arrival, others have tiered openings where only select grades report on the first day. In some middle and high schools, students' schedules are distributed to students on the first day. I know of school districts that are required to distribute all textbooks on day one, and more parents attend school on the first day of school than any other day of the school year. Regardless of what is occurring in the school, parents expect to see a principal who is in control of his surroundings and willing to provide answers to a variety of questions like "why was my child not promoted" to "is it possible to have my daughter placed in Ms. Jackson's class?" To give parents the time they deserve in answering these questions, consider setting up individual conferences after the workday or the following day. When parents ask impromptu questions, they actually have the advantage since they have thought through the questions time and again before posing them to you. No matter the complexity of tasks required for a smooth day one, a new principal will be judged strongly based on the success of that day.

The first day of school will be filled with anxiety from students, teachers, parents, and administrators. An effective principal plans and prepares his or her staff to minimize the levels of anxiety. The principal must be the captain of the ship. From registering students to the dismissal of classes, the principal must have first hand knowledge of every operation of the first day. As with any solid system, the principal must have intimate knowledge of the operation; however, the success of the operation or system should not rely upon the principal's participation. The principal must delegate first day tasks to staff and work to support their efforts. The principal will be too busy to dedicate his or her time to any single task. To give you an idea of the principal's demands on the first day, I will reflect on one of my many first days of school.

My Day One

In August of 2008, I served as a principal who led a transformation of a junior high school into a pre-kindergarten through eighth grade school. Due to the political environment of the city and school system, I felt the whole city was watching to see if the first day would be successful. Upon my arrival at approximately 7:15 a.m., there was a bulldozer in front of the door that my younger students were slated to use to enter the building. The bulldozer was used during the construction of the playground over the summer. With the parents of the students arriving in less than one hour, I demanded the contractors move the tractor. Fortunately, the move was coordinated and completed in enough time to avoid local news cameras from filming the unsightly machine on school property. While a bulldozer in front of the school is nothing in isolation, if news cameras had discovered other issues on opening day, the bulldozer may have supported the notion of the school not being in an appropriate state to open.

At 8:00 a.m., students began entering the building for breakfast. To separate the upper and lower school populations, we utilized two different entrances for students to enter the building. Students in grades pre-kindergarten through fifth used one entrance and grades six through eight used a separate entrance. This was done to calm parents' fears regarding young students interacting with older students while in school. The routine for lower school students was for them to report to the auditorium after breakfast and sit with their classmates. At 8:40, teachers met their classes in the auditorium and escort them to the classroom. When the upper school students arrived, staff members were present to inform them of their homeroom classes and room numbers. Additional staff members were positioned on the floors where the upper school students' classrooms were located to provide additional support and minimize loitering. Once in homeroom, students received their daily class schedule. While these separate operations of moving students to class were occurring, approximately 40 parents were enrolling and withdrawing students to and from the school. While some school districts require parents to complete the enrollment process much earlier, the district in which I worked did not require parents to do so, creating another operation to plan for on day one. By 9:25, the process of placing all students into class concluded.

Since it was the first day of school after highly publicized school closings, I did not know what to expect. At approximately 10:00 a.m., while the building was still swarming with parents, news reporters with cameras in tow appeared at the front door. My experience with news cameras has generally been unsatisfactory. Reporters tend to look for stories that capture shortcomings of the school. On this day, everything school related was well planned and being effectively executed. As a result, a "story" of my school was never broadcast on the news. Had something gone wrong that day, I can only imagine that the outcome would have been different. And the worse the issue, the more news coverage it would have received. The fact that the local news appeared at the school caused anxiety amongst the staff. Unpredictable events are common as a principal; however, it supports the importance of having a thorough plan. Planning is critical. By 10:30, the reporters departed.

At approximately 11:00, the superintendent/chancellor appeared. Of course, her arrival was unannounced. To my surprise, the chancellor was accompanied by at least six news reporters and cameras. By this time, many of the parents who were present to oversee day one, felt comfortable enough to leave. The chancellor toured the building, entered several classrooms, and spoke to several students. While her visit was welcomed, her entourage did cause a bit of confusion. The chancellor departed by 11:30 and the day resumed as planned.

At 11:45, lunches began. My school had three lunch periods. This specific year, food services implemented a new system to better account for lunches. The system required all students to enter a nine-digit code, regardless of their age. Our school served students from pre-kindergarten through eighth grade, and the expectation was that three-year-old students were expected to input their special code. For younger students, the process did not go as smoothly as it did for our sixth through eighth grade students. The goal was to keep our lunches on schedule. Failing to feed students in a timely manner interferes with the schedule of everyone within the building.

At approximately 1:15, my assistant superintendent, who was my immediate supervisor, appeared in the school. Like all the other guests, he expected to be given a tour of the building. Fortunately, due to the nature of the summer construction that occurred, I had been in close communication with him through the entire summer. He was well aware of the fact that our library was non-existent, some classrooms were without chalk boards, and some teachers' supplies had yet to arrive. Therefore, the nature of his tour was different than that of the chancellor, who had news cameras in tow. While I could have exposed the school for its deficiencies that I had been fighting with central office all summer to correct, it would have been a negative reflection on the school. These are the types of decisions that you will need to make as a principal. Your actions will be under constant scrutiny, so proceed wisely. Since my assistant superintendent had a comprehensive under-standing of the school, his visit was brief. He departed by 1:30.

After my supervisor's departure, there was just enough time for a quick lunch and time to prepare for dismissal. Parents are very anxious on the first day of school. Even though we discussed dismissal procedures with parents during student/parent orientations, parents still insisted on retrieving students from classrooms. According to our plan, students would be dismissed through two doors on opposite sides of the building. To help support our plan, I had staff members stationed at the doors, explaining the dismissal process to parents. At 3:00, dismissal began. The teachers escorted their students to the appropriate door. As planned, parents waited to retrieve their students outside the school. At 3:30, the dismissal was complete.

At 4:00, I met with team leaders to share feedback regarding the first day. This meeting included a discussion about the logistics of tasks that needed to occur over the next few days including textbook and locker distribution. We also discussed if we needed to modify the schedule for ensuing days. Since the day was well planned and effectively executed, this meeting was uneventful, but necessary.

At 4:30, I begin to call parents who requested to meet with me that morning. These meetings generally related to retained students, summer school issues, or teacher requests. As a rule of thumb, always start these meetings in an optimistic mood. Undoubtedly, you will have to work with these parents throughout the year so start on a good note. This first round of phone calls and conferences lasted until 5:45. Having finished the first round, I had to proceed to the next task.

At 6:00, I met with the head of the maintenance team to conduct a walk-through of the facility. This is the first day the building is subjected to the wear and tear of children. On day one, it is important to set the standard of cleanliness for when students are in the building. Inspect bathrooms, classrooms, hallways, etc. Let the maintenance department know what is an acceptable level of cleanliness. In my school, I hated to see graffiti on walls and lockers. In addition, I hated to see litter or chewing gum on floors. I felt that these were signs of a lazy maintenance team, but it was my responsibility to set the standard. At approximately 7:00, I completed my walk through and returned to my office.

As a principal, you will find that it is very difficult to complete your own tasks throughout the workday. At 7:00 p.m. on day one, I made some notes about things that needed to happen during the following days and answered approximately 15 emails. Before leaving at 8:00, I returned several phone calls. While day one was a long day, it was truly a success.

Healthy Routines and Rituals

One of the most critical components to any school is the creation of healthy routines and rituals. I have served as the principal with staffs as small as 40 and as large as 95. Regardless of the size of your staff, you must create healthy routines within your building to support your work. From the first day of school, you need to create as many useful routines as possible. For example, teacher leave, class coverage, class visits, and visitors in the building are all things that appear to be minor in nature. However, when you have three teachers who call in sick and you have to create coverage for their students, a system is required. In most schools, visitors (parents) are encouraged to visit classrooms. However, what is the procedure for parents visiting classrooms? Do parents need to stop by the office before they report to class? Can parents talk to their child or the teacher during visits? Can parents remove their child without returning to the office? These questions may appear to lack worth until a child is removed by a parent who has a court order denying them access to their child. The more healthy routines you implement, the easier it will be to manage the school. You will simply have to manage the systems, not each person within the school.

After systems have been established, you now have a responsibility to start "watching." The art of watching will play a critical role in your ability to gain a deep understanding of your organization. Watching is just that, watching. You do not need to share your observations with staff members. As a new principal, you will surely need to develop your own opinions regarding staff in your school. When I became the princi-pal of my last school, I walked the halls peering into classrooms, nurse's suite, counselor's office, etc., just to get an idea of the daily operation of the school. I rarely shared information from these walks, but rather gathered information on my new school. As you walk the building it is important for you to observe how staff is interacting with each other, parents, and students. Watching should include monitoring the upkeep of the facility. Before major change can occur within the school, the principal must understand the inner workings of the school. This understanding generally occurs in one of two ways-listening to staff, parent, and student reports, or making your own observations. The two ways are not completely independent of each other; however, accepting all information provided by staff as absolute truth will often result in the acceptance of their personal perceptions about events in the school. As a new principal, you will surely need to develop your own opinions regarding staff in your school-- do this by simply watching.

*   *   *   *   *

SCENARIO

When a new principal is selected or appointed to a school, some people view this change of leadership as an opportunity. If the former principal served in that position for an extended period of time, they probably formed relationships with specific vendors, community people, service providers, parents, etc. As I began my principalship in one of my schools, people were coming from far and wide, offering my students "the world." At the time, unbeknownst to me, the former principal maintained only a few partnerships for a reason. When my predecessor was serving as principal, she quickly and quietly dismissed any person outside the network of people with whom she had pre-existing relation-ships. Because of my open door approach to all, with the goal of devel-oping business partnerships, I learned of peoples' greed and promotion of personal agendas the hard way. At times, there are inherent, divergent interests. Outside agencies are often interested in making money from schools, while schools are interested in educating students. Many outside agencies hide their true purpose under the guise of education. When I was faced with this situation, I tried to assess the true worth of what was proposed by the seller. During the proposal period, specifically ask--how will your services help my students? What is the expense or staff commitment required by the school? Are these services really worth the school's commitment?

Questions to Consider:

- How should principals sort through the numerous outside agencies that are attempting to provide services to your students?
- Does it make a difference if a parent of a student is serving as a representative for the agency?
- How do you decide which outside agencies/community representatives should be taken seriously?

CHAPTER 4

September

Chapter 4 includes the following subjects:
- Public Relations
- Conducting Initial Instructional Assessments
- Identifying "Target" Student Populations
- Back to School Night
- Gaining an Understanding of the Critical Areas in the School

Whether your school year starts in August or September, September will be the first month that you will work in its entirety. With the events of August having already been set in stone, you have to look to maximize September. If, for whatever reason, things did not go as planned in August, September is a month that can be used to correct unforeseen events that occurred. By the end of September, you should have a very good working knowledge of your entire staff. Use this to your advantage.

Generally, for a new principal, September will serve as the honeymoon period. Even though the honeymoon period provides a level of flexibility that may not exist six months later, do act hastily with the implementation of new policies and practices. With limited knowledge of the inner workings of the school, it is easy to make erroneous judgments that result in costly mistakes. It is more important to make informed decisions later in the year than rushing to take advantage of the honeymoon period.

Public Relations

Regardless of the condition of the school when you became principal, the leadership change alone can support a public relations campaign. It is critical to get your staff to understand the role they play in the public relations as it relates to the school. Negative and positive stories are generally rooted in information provided by the staff. The staff must understand its role in creating positive publicity regarding the workplace. This is especially true in schools that have an extensive history of negative publicity. In such circumstances, the principal must articulate the importance for staff to share positive information about the school. After all, if staff members repeatedly bash the school publicly, it inevitably becomes a negative reflection of all the staff within the school. The staff must be positive in the public relation game.

As a new principal, you may ask about ways to generate positive publicity for the school. Within the school, monthly newsletters, school calendars, and phone calls may be made highlighting positive activities that have occurred throughout the month. In addition, school web pages that include exciting occurrences should be maintained and updated on a regular basis. In addition, it is critical that you publicly acknowledge students for excelling academically, athletically, etc. This public recognition provides parents with information to rave about to their friends within the community. As a new principal, understand the potential of your new role. As for positive public relations, use your new role to generate momentum.

Aside from orientations that occurred before the start of the school year, the "Back to School" Night will probably be the first opportunity to highlight positive events that occurred since the start of the school year. Take advantage of this opportunity by highlighting students and staff members. Parents love seeing their children being portrayed in a positive light. In addition, students can help to present events that have occurred in school. For the teachers, parents want to hear that their children's teacher is being recognized for being effective. Within the Back to School event, carve out time for parents to interact with teachers. Essentially, your Back to School Night will serve as a major public relations event.

The principalship is very much like a game of chess. In fact, most decisions will require you to make minor or major staff changes. For example, many states have an "official count" day in early September in which students are actually counted. The total enrollment, based on this count, determines a school's funding amount. Because of an over estimate between the projected and actual number of students, a reduction of staff may need to occur. With this in mind, staff moves may be required as early as mid-September. As a new leader, you will be responsible for orchestrating this process so it is in your best interests to know the strengths and weaknesses of each of your staff members. Staff moves may come in the form of layoffs, in-house transfers, grade level changes, etc. The decisions that are often difficult for veteran principals are even more difficult for your less inexperienced colleagues (or peers),   especially when you consider that the new principal had less than six weeks to assess the skills of his staff. In preparation for unforeseen situations like this, it is critical that the new principal begin to assess the staff from the first day of school, if not the first day of starting the job.

More often than not, you will be required to make staff changes in the middle of the school year. This could happen because of the long-term illness of a staff member, pregnancy, resignation, etc. As a principal, you will be amazed by the situations that you are confronted with at the most inopportune moments, but as the leader, you are still expected to effectively lead the school. Having a comprehensive understanding of the strengths and weaknesses of your staff will contribute to your success as a leader. In the event that you need to cover for a fourth grade math teacher from December through June, you need to know what teachers in your school excel at math and what teachers may have taught fourth grade in the past. You would also need to understand the level of cooperation and willingness that each teacher has to support their school. As a principal, these types of decisions may occur a few times a year. The principal's understanding of the staff will be the key to leading the school through these challenging times.

One of the ways to gain an understanding of your teaching staff is to conduct informal instructional observations very early. While some teacher contracts prevent official observations from beginning as late as October 1, you must conduct unofficial observations from the first week of school. Classroom visits, especially early in the school year, do not need long narratives explaining what you observed. If feedback is necessary, feel free to use checklists or rubrics. If distributed before the informal observations, these checklists can be used to reinforce expectations. For the first few weeks of school, I recommend the principal make daily classroom visits to each classroom. Within a week, patterns in teachers will begin to form, providing the principal with sound knowledge about each teacher. The information generated from these visits can serve as the basis for staffing decisions.

Just as you need to gain an understanding of teachers, you will also need to gain an understanding of students. Depending on the grade levels served by the school, an academic assessment should be conducted within the first few weeks of the school year. While the principal has had access to school, grade, or class-level data from the previous year, an instructional assessment would provide current student-level data. This could prove to be very important if two classes needed to be merged or a parent requested a teacher change for a student. With current student level data, those decisions can be supported by data, as opposed to opinions alone. In addition, early academic assessments serve as benchmarks for teacher performance. It is very difficult to hold teachers accountable for student achievement when the first benchmark data is not generated until October or November. Early assessments identify student achievement and teacher performance data from the start of the year.

While less than desirable, you may be required to separate or merge classes during the month of September. This may occur because of enrollment projections that prove to be false. When merging or separating classes, I would encourage you to consider the strengths and weaknesses of both the staff and students. Whenever possible, I would encourage input from students' current teachers. More times than not, they will possess greater insight into students' character traits and are more than capable of creating class rosters that will be successful. The process of altering classes in the middle of the school year can be difficult; however, utilizing staff to support this process eases the immense challenge of the task.

If current educational trends continue, high-stakes testing will continue to play a critical role in our schools. With this in mind, it is in your best interests to hire or retain an effective testing coordinator and a testing committee. With the volume of information required to administer a standardized test, it is critical to have an effective standardized testing coordinator on staff. The current process of coding and organizing test booklets would overburden a principal while trying to maintain the school. To support the coordinator, one may consider creating an entire testing team. While the coordinator is ultimately responsible for the testing plan, the committee would provide clear communication lines to the remainder of the staff. In addition, with many current standardized testing programs including several benchmark tests, testing procedures would need to be organized and executed multiple times throughout the year. The testing person, supported by the testing committee, must be ready to support the process.

The current data-driven culture that exists within many schools will result in numerous assessments throughout the year. Each test will require the disaggregation of data that impact the instructional program in a variety of ways. While an assistant principal or counselor can work together to complete all of the tasks associated with a school's comprehensive program, it may be in the best interests of the school to hire a person to support this process. Depending on the testing demands of the school, a part-time position may be able to adequately complete these tasks. Generally, graphs need to be generated so the data can be presented to the larger staff. Frequently, the typical people who are assigned to these tasks do not possess the knowledge to excel in this arena. If your school's budget can support this type of person, hire a testing coordinator.

*   *   *   *   *

SCENARIO

When leading a school, you will have all types of people who work for you. If you work in public schools, as I have for the vast majority of my career, the range of the types of people may be wider. After serving as a principal for several years, very few situations surprised me. On a September morning after Back to School Night, I had a parent approach me. She confronted me in the front of the school. She was visibly angry and insisted that her daughter be transferred from one class to another. Not knowing the details behind her demand and trying to avoid any undue attention, I requested that she come into my office. Once in my office, she stated that her daughter's teacher was a homosexual and she did not agree with that lifestyle. As a result, she insisted that her daughter be transferred immediately. Of course, I did not authorize a transfer solely based on the sexuality of the teacher. I told the parent that I could not confirm the sexuality of the teacher. In addition, I shared that the teacher was outstanding and I was sure that her daughter would thrive both academically and socially throughout the year. The mother stated that her religious beliefs did not support homosexuality and her daughter's wholesome thoughts would be tainted by the daily teacher/student interactions. The mother threatened to withdraw her daughter from the school if the transfer was not executed. For the record, I never transferred the student.

Questions to Consider:

- What are the pros and cons of complying with the parent's request?
- Is it legal to transfer a student from one class to another solely based on the sexuality of the teacher?
- Would you share the parents' transfer request (and all associated information) with the teacher?

CHAPTER 5

October

Chapter 5 includes the following subjects:
- Goal Setting Conferences
- Preparing for the First Parent Teacher Conferences
- Avenues for Communication
- Instructional Assessments
- Understanding Staff/Administration Dynamics
- Revisiting the Master Schedule

The school year will begin to settle during the month of October. As the principal, you will begin to see patterns with staff, students, parents, etc. The patterns provide insight into the strengths and weaknesses of the organization. For example, if the third grade teacher is writing an excessive amount of student referrals during period six, it is in the best interests of the principal to understand the reasons for the high number of referrals at this time. As opposed to August and September, October provides historical data via patterns of behaviors. As a principal, it is much easier to address a pattern of behaviors than a single incident.

While you are observing your staff and students for patterns, understand that they are also observing you. By October, everyone in the school understands the frequency in which the principal visits classrooms or if staff is permitted to report to work late. Armed with this knowledge, it is critical that the principal model expected behaviors.

Goal Setting

I realize that schools and teachers are required to establish school goals in the beginning of the school year; however, by October, the newly appointed principal should have a realistic understanding of the goals of the school. This understanding allows the principal to extend his expectations to individual staff members. To hold staff members accountable for achieving individual and school goals, individual meetings should be held with all staff members to clarify the purpose and objective of the organization. If these meetings are held in August or September, the principal does not possess enough information to have informed conversations with the staff.

Depending on the school calendar, the first parent teacher conferences will occur during the month of October. Just like Back to School Night, the first parent teacher conference can be used to promote good things that are occurring in the school. Encourage teachers to display current work both inside and outside the classrooms and make sure the entire facility is in top shape. As parents move about the building, they will surely be informally inspecting the building, especially the restrooms. This may be the first opportunity that parents have to walk through the building without school being in session.

As the new principal, do not take for granted that teachers know how to conduct parent teacher conferences. Sometimes, even veteran teachers need to be reminded of the purpose of parent teacher conferences. The desired uniformity of the these conferences may serve as a reference point for all parent conferences throughout the school year. I generally required teachers to start the conversation with a positive fact regarding the student. In addition, I required teachers to provide a portfolio of work that reflected the status of each child. When speaking of deficiencies of a child, I expected the teacher to offer suggestions to the parent to address the child's needs. I never wanted children to be characterized as too needy and have the teacher not willing to provide solutions to the problem. Like a teacher over-preparing for the first day of school, the principal should over-prepare for the first parent-teacher conference day.

The first parent teacher conference day is also a perfect time to look for parent volunteers to fill various positions throughout the building; however, be strategic with placing your volunteers. Since you are beginning to gain an understanding of the school, you should begin to know your exact needs. Parents as volunteers can fill various voids throughout the building; free help is not always good help. While volunteers can be useful, you must always be careful where they are assigned. Schools have high volumes of confidential information. It is the responsibility of the principal to ensure that volunteers do not have access to confidential information. Keep this in mind as you prepare to solicit volunteers. The potential for their positive impact on the school environment is likely; however, the ineffective use of volunteers can prove to have a detrimental impact on the school and principal.

With over a month of positive events happening within the school, October is a great month to begin to send home newsletters, calendars, etc. While some schools begin sending home generic materials from the first day of school, the "take-home" materials can begin to reflect actual events that have occurred in the school during the entire month of September. What is more important than the actual materials that are sent home is the regularity in which materials are distributed. For example, if your school sends a monthly calendar home the last week of each month for the ensuing month, then parents come to expect that form of communication at that time every month. If the communication patterns are established, then any information that would be of interest to the parents can be included with the calendar. Some schools use "Tuesday Notes" as a way to communicate with parents. Using this method, the school sends pertinent information to parents every

Tuesday. Whatever method you choose to communicate with parents, understand that October will be the month where communication patterns are formed.

Due to the No Child Left Behind Act of 2001, schools have become very data driven. The test-taking culture, regardless whether you agree with it or not, is characteristic of the current situation in education. As a result, it is in the best interests of the school to create another academic data point in October. When comparing October's data to September's data, you should be able to begin to assess your staff's strengths and weaknesses. While this data may be telling, remember that the year is still early and your staff has room to grow. You may want to meet with your teachers to discuss the results of the data and rearticulate your instructional vision of the school.

Depending on your school district and your student enrollment numbers on "Count Day," you may be required to make modifications during the month of October, adding or reducing staff members. In the worst-case scenario, you will need to cut teachers. In some districts, these decisions will be based entirely on staff seniority, while other districts allow principals to make these decisions based on performance. Teachers' union contracts generally drive this process. By October, the principal is expected to understand the inner workings of the school to make the "right" decision.

October is also a good time to review your school's master schedule. Whether you had the privilege of creating the master schedule or you just inherited it from your predecessor, you should be able to alter it to better suit your students' needs. In the event that you were forced to add or reduce the number of teachers, you may be required to modify your master schedule. Remember, your master schedule provides the framework for students to receive instruction. The creation or modification of the master schedule is a thoughtful process. Use all points of data to make the most informed decisions when optimizing the master schedule.

*   *   *   *   *

SCENARIO

In the role of the principal, you can never anticipate what will happen on a given day. Late one morning in October, I was in the middle of supervising a lunch period when a call came over my walkie-talkie (radio). The call requested that I report to the main office immediately. Of course I wanted to know more about the situation; however, we never provided sensitive information over administrative radios. As I approached the main office, I heard students crying, coughing, and running through the hallways. When I reached the main office, police officers were entering the building. Reportedly, a student dispensed a canister of tear gas on the third floor. The irritant entered the ventilation system and quickly began to impact the entire third floor and parts of the second floor. To effectively treat affected students, we created a triage area on the front lawn. Due to the mysterious nature of the situation, students, staff, and parents were very anxious for answers. After the fire and police department officials authorized staff and students to return to the building, we held a quick briefing to dispel any false information associated with the incident. The incident lasted for approximately two hours and then it was back to business as usual.

Questions to Consider:

-   What is the appropriate protocol for staff (other than the principal) contacting the police and fire department?
-   How should you notify the parents of this event?
-   In moving forward, how do you address your student body to prevent this from happening again?

CHAPTER 6

November

Chapter 6 includes the following subjects:
- First Report Cards
- The Ranking of Teachers
- Celebrating Staff and Student Victories
- Planning the School Budget
- Inclement Weather Procedures

November is the first month where you should be able to reap the rewards of your early work. By November, the routines and rituals should be firmly in place. In addition, you should have conducted multiple classroom observations and target conferences with teachers. By November, you probably would have made several big decisions for the well being of the school. Take time to assess the current condition of the school as compared to its condition in July.

November is generally the time in which report cards are distributed for the first marking period. As the principal, you must be mindful of the first report cards. Contrary to popular belief, teachers use these report cards to send various messages to students and parents. For instance, some teachers purposely give students a lower grade to serve as motivation or send a message to a student that there is still room for growth. On the other extreme, teachers sometimes give students passing grades when they are actually failing in an attempt to raise a student's self-esteem. The principal must examine report card data to address grading trends and calibrate the grading system of the school. Especially for the first report card, principals must check teachers' comments on report cards. Some may argue that comments provide greater insight into a student's performance as compared to absolute grades. Principals must make sure that report card comments are in line with the overall mission of the school and district. A word to the wise--address report card issues early, it will save precious time as later report cards are generated.

While November seems a bit early to begin thinking about the following year, it is actually the time to begin assessing teachers' talents with the goal of formulating effective teaching teams for the following year. Starting this process in November allows you to think about various scenarios that the teachers will face as the year progresses. When thinking of different team combinations, you must see how teachers respond to various challenges throughout the year. If you start this process too late, you will fail to gain a comprehensive understanding of the possible strengths and weaknesses of each teacher.

By November, the newness of the school year has faded. Both teachers and students will begin to feel worn down. As the principal, it is important to remain upbeat during this period. Even though teachers have been working for 2-3 two-to-three months, the road ahead is still long. In November, teachers sometimes get the feeling that "this thing is never going to end." To help overcome this feeling, the principal must celebrate authentic teacher victories within the school. These celebrations could include perfect teacher attendance, recognition for committee participation, exemplary teacher performance regarding student achievement, etc. Teachers enjoy being recognized and your acknowledgement of their commitment will serve as motivation for the coming months.

One of the major public relations opportunities that you will have is the holiday program. For religious reasons, I would use the term holiday as opposed to Christmas program. Even if the majority of your school community is Christian, the term holiday program is more inclusive. To effectively plan for this program, preparation must begin in November. The goal of the program is to showcase the students of your school. You may want to consider having band, chorus, dramatic, or dance performances. In the absence of these groups, you may want to have individual classes present poetry or display artwork in a makeshift gallery. These are only suggestions. By November, you will be in a position to know how to highlight students' talents in your school. To increase the chances of a successful program, plan early.

School budgets can be very tricky. The dollar amounts you are promised in August are often different than your budget total in November. Due to the reconciliation of grant money and student enrollment numbers, the dollar amount within the school's budget will fluctuate a bit. It is important to remember that the budget is only a projection until October/November. Even after that point, there may still be modifications. November is a good time to create a spending plan for the remainder of the school year. Oftentimes, school districts require a spending plan to be completed in August or September; however, I found that dollar amounts change so much during the first few months that this practice is pointless. November's spending plan should be comprehensive in nature, but leave room for unanticipated purchases. As a principal of a building, you will never be able to anticipate the needs of every teacher and child within your school.

Depending on where your school is located, November is typically the last month of predictable weather. From December through March, the potential for snow days becomes a reality. While teachers and students love snow days, they can create real issues for administrators, especially when a snow plan does not exist. November is the perfect time to review snow plans. As the principal, you must ensure that your school's walkways and steps are free of ice and snow. While you probably have a building service manager or custodial foreman who oversees the process of snow and ice removal, the principal will ultimately be held responsible for any incidents that occur due to hazardous situations. The snow plan must provide details as to how and who is responsible for removing snow and the logistics regarding the notification of students, parents, and staff of the closing or modified schedule of the school.

*   *   *   *   *

SCENARIO

Schools are no different than other places of work. Like supervisors of small corporations, principals are responsible for a relatively large number of employees. Depending on the size of the school, principals could be responsible for hundreds of employees, many of whom do not have the students' interests as a priority. While serving as the principal of an intermediate school, I had a teacher who repeatedly attempted to concoct stories to gain placement on administrative leave. For example, in November, she stated that a student hit her with a book by throwing it at her. Even though she claimed the book hit her in the face, she could not immediately identify the student who threw the book. To make matters worse, the students could not confirm the story of a student throwing the book. The teacher reported the alleged incident to the teacher's union and claimed that I did not take actions against the students, even though the teacher failed to identify the responsible student or group of students. After the teacher's union representative stated that she would have to identify a student for disciplinary actions to be executed, the teacher accused a female student of the act. The student who was accused had attended the school for a number of years and had a spotless behavioral track record. The teacher, with the backing of the teacher's union, insisted that the teacher be placed on a 10-day, paid administrative leave and the student be expelled. When I took all of the factors into consideration, I did not support either position set forth by the teacher's union. I felt that the teacher, who was a terrible teacher, was attempting to cheat the school system at the expense of an innocent student. I simply could not support these actions. Even though the union backed the teacher, the teacher decided not to pursue a grievance against me.

Questions to Consider

- What are the pros and cons against supporting the teacher's claims?
- What factors needed to be taken into consideration when making the decision to pursue or not pursue actions against the student?
- Could I have made alternate decisions that would have appeased the teacher?

CHAPTER 7

December

Chapter 7 includes the following subjects:
- Winter Break Preparation
- The Holiday Program
- Preplanning for the following school year
- Identifying Cohorts for Standardized tests
- Winter Break Work Schedule

As a principal, I always believed that if staff members stayed until December, I could convince them to stay until the end of the school year. New teachers, not knowing how difficult the job of teaching would be when they accepted the position, are more likely to quit before December. December, widely regarded as the mid point of the year, is a milestone for your entire staff. In most districts, winter break is the first extended break of the school year. It is a well-deserved time to regroup for the second half of the school year.

In planning for the break, holiday packets should be provided to every student. You surely do not want the skills that your students learned from August to be forgotten over the winter break. In addition, when parents help their children with the completion of these assignments, they will gain insight into topics being covered in school. If you view work packets as an archaic method for supplying work over the break, many schools encourage students to use various websites. Some of these programs are a component of a school's regular instructional program while others are simply websites that the school endorses. Just remember that programs used by the school typically require users to input a special password to access the site. To address this challenge, you should probably provide a list of school approved websites and include passwords before the start of winter break.

The planning of the holiday program that started in November should now be completed. The holiday program serves as a highlight for the first half of the school year. With parents, students, and staff members all being excited, take advantage of the moment by having an outstanding program. If you are not completely sure how the program will be executed, conduct a dry run of the program during the day. This is commonly done in front of the student body before the parents are shown the program. As with any dry run, this allows the kinks to be corrected. In addition, it allows the principal to view the entire show before the evening performance. As a principal, I generally had evening performances to provide parents the opportunity to see their son or daughter perform without taking leave from work. The holiday program is a great opportunity to generate positive publicity for the school.

In an earlier chapter, I discussed the importance of selecting school-based leadership in half-year terms. December is the month that you should decide on the next group of school-based leaders. By this juncture in the school year, you will have a comprehensive understanding of your staff and be more than capable of identifying the next leaders. Even though these leaders will not be implemented until January, the next group of leaders should be notified in December. This provides them with ample time to prepare for their new role. In addition, it allows the principal time to discuss the selections with the new leaders. These roles may include team leaders, department chairpersons, grade level coordinators, etc.

Just as the principal should have a thorough understanding of staff, teachers should have a thorough understanding of their students' academic standings. In December, teachers should begin to notify parents about students who are being considered for retention. While some school districts require an official parent notification by March 1, realistically, this date is too late to provide significant interventions to improve the chances of the child's promotion. A December notification allows parents to register their child in tutorial services, after school programs, and other supplemental supports that may result in the drastic improvement of the child's academic status. Due to the seriousness of student retentions, I would recommend having an official conference with parents when student retentions are being considered.

In the current education world of high-stakes testing, you should consider an intensive support program. If you have not already implemented a program before December, you should strongly consider doing so before the winter break. A December start allows you to get a thorough understanding of the scope of the program. To begin the planning phase, you need to determine the students that you want to target. After you determine the target group, you must identify the appropriate staff to execute the program. After you determine the students and staff, you must determine the curriculum or instructional materials needed to make the program successful. Completing these tasks by December still allows enough time to focus the efforts of the supplemental program to maximize student achievement. If bolstering student achievement for the statewide standardized test is the goal of your program, your supplemental program needs to be started no later than December (assuming the test is in March/April).

As previously stated, winter break is the first substantive break of the school year. Depending on the school district in which you work, this break looks very different. In some districts, all staff are also on leave. In other districts, office staff and custodians are required to work, but not teachers. In yet other districts, teachers are required to participate in professional development activities. Regardless of the situation, the principal will need to plan for winter break. In my experiences as a principal, the custodians need to conduct a thorough cleaning of the facility, office staff can file documents and prepare for the spring, and teachers can prepare lessons for their return. Whatever the case, winter break will require a plan. Do not allow the break to pass without making progress.

*   *   *   *   *

SCENARIO

As the principal, I often found myself the bearer of more information than I desired to have. Parents, teachers, and students tend to share tremendous amounts of information with the principal. Unfortunately, much of the information is of a confidential nature. This information cannot be readily shared. This sometimes causes problems when working to protect the student from situations in which teachers do not have the same insight. For example, I had an elementary student whose teachers repeatedly reported him for "acting out." Simply put, teachers wanted the student disciplined severely. Having spoken to his mother, she shared that the parents were in the midst of an ugly divorce and the father recently disappeared from his son's life. She asked me not to share the details with his teachers. Trying to respect the wishes of his mother, I simply told teachers to be sensitive to the student's needs because he was experiencing very difficult times at home. The teachers, not knowing the severity of the issues, insisted that the student be disciplined for his actions; however, possessing the information that I knew, I could not punish the student for causing issues. To address the student's needs, I scheduled a meeting with all of his teachers, school counselor, nurse, and assistant principal. During the meeting, the mother disclosed the recent family history to the team. The information was so troubling that the staff took an entirely different approach to the student. The mother shared that she had recently told her son that the husband was not actually the boy's father. She lost her $45,000/year job and was now living on \$330/month, and they would probably be moving to a shelter in the near future. She also admitted that her son had been urinating and defecating around the house for the last five months. The student had been stealing money from his mother and selling goods from the house to make money. At the conclusion of the meeting, there was not a dry eye in the room. As a school, we had a responsibility to pour all of our resources into both the student and family to help his situation. Equipped with this information, the teachers were more than willing to provide support to the student, as opposed to administering severe disciplinary actions.

Questions to Consider

- Does the principal have a responsibility to the parent to keep information confidential, even if it negatively impacts the student's educational process?
- How do you balance (decide? Choose? Determine? ??)what information to share with your staff?
- Is it acceptable to tell parents, students, and staff that you do not want to hear any additional information?

CHAPTER 8

January

Chapter 8 includes the following subjects:
- -Revisiting the School's Goals
- Focusing on the Standardized Test
- Planning for the Following Year
- Mid-Year Changes
- Re-establishing Routines and Rituals
- Mid Year Conferences

A s with the start of the school year in August, January will lend itself to implementing new initiatives and setting additional goals as a staff. Some people consider January to be a mini honeymoon period. Both teachers and students return to school energized. As for the principal, you probably worked over the break but are ready to start the new calendar year.

An effective way to maintain focus upon your staff's return is to revisit the school's goals for both teachers and students. You may revisit school goals by conducting individual classroom visits or large group assemblies; each way has its advantage. By presenting in a large assembly, all teachers and students receive a single message. Presenting to individual classes allows for dialogue between administrators, teachers, and students that may not be possible during schoolwide assemblies. You will need to determine which method suits your school's setting the best. Either large assemblies or small group meetings will support your objective of reemphasizing the goals of the school.

In addition to meeting with staff and students together, you may want to conduct individual conferences with teachers. The conference could be used for a variety of purposes including the review of performance data and goal setting for the remainder of the school year. By meeting with the teacher, the conference serves a dual purpose. Individual conferences allow the teacher to voice his opinion and they provide an opportunity for the principal to provide "midseason" feedback to the teacher.

Remember, the routines and rituals that you established serve as the foundation of your school. For whatever reason, the weeklong winter break can result in a temporary amnesia for both students and staff. As the principal, it is critical that you revisit the importance of maintaining healthy routines and rituals within the school. You will need to lead this initiative. One way to ensure that routines and rituals are being followed is to model desired behavior at all times. If this does not work, you will probably need to document behaviors via letters to the teachers. Students who do not comply with expectations will have to be disciplined. The focus on healthy routines and rituals will result in a successful second half of the school year.

If standardized tests continue to have the same importance as they do in today's educational framework, the principal must ensure that a student's performance on the statewide test is an authentic goal and focal point of the school. When I think of a school's preparation for standardized tests, I compare it to approaching a pothole while driving a car. When approaching a pothole at a moderate pace, the driver will often do one of two things. After identifying the exact location of the pothole, the driver will either swerve to avoid the pothole or figuratively close his eyes and wish for the best. When preparing for the standardized test, the principal can either lead the initiative of effectively preparing for the test, or close his eyes and let fate run its course. When it comes to leading schools, preparation is always better than fate. If you are the principal of a school that has a history of failing to meet academic targets on standardized tests, you must create a systematic plan to increase students' performances on these tests. Not only will you need to make sure the content of the test is being covered, you also need to develop a winning mindset in all of the stakeholders of the school. If you are in a school that has historically achieved academic targets, you will still need to have a plan for maintaining or improving the academic success of the school. You would hate to be the principal who is perceived as a failure, simply because you did not achieve the academic targets on the standardized test.

January is a great time to make changes in the school. Whether they are staff assignments, duties, student sections, etc, the return after winter break lends itself to such changes. While the staff does not always perceive change as a positive event, as long as you are transparent in your decisions, and your decisions support the betterment of students in the school, then change will eventually be accepted. With the newness of the new calendar year and the revitalization of staff, January is the perfect time to make changes.

As indicated throughout the book, the principal must be forward thinking and plot the course of the school. With this in mind, the principal must begin planning for the following school year in January. This allows the principal to take advantage of planning opportunities that were not available. January thoughts that you exercise in January should revolve around master schedule changes, teacher assignments, room assignments, and hiring needs. These may seem like minor details; however, these areas will serve as your foundation in moving the school forward. Do not forego the opportunity to plan early.

*　　*　　*　　*　　*

SCENARIO

In January of 2007, as I was trying to recover from an unplanned snow day, I received a call over the radio. The original call was not for me; however, the nature of the dialogue led me to believe that there was a serious situation developing in the auditorium. During a rehearsal that was being conducted in the auditorium, a first grade student got her arm stuck in the side of a chair. The calls over the radio were requesting the custodian, nurse, and assistant principal report to the auditorium immediately. After hearing the requests, I reported to the auditorium. When I arrived, the student was yelling. It was clear that she was in a great deal of pain. Her arm was positioned in a way that there was no clear solution to freeing it without causing more harm. As each person arrived, it was obvious that nobody had an answer to the problem. To make matters worse, there were approximately 75 students who were also panicking. After clearing the auditorium of everyone but five adults, we quietly examined the situation. After a few moments, we decided to disassemble the chair. Even though this process took 10-15 minutes, it seemed to be the only viable solution. I didn't want to destroy the chair since I knew the school district would never fix or replace it. The chair was disassembled and the student's arm was removed without any damage. For me, that was a win-win situation.

Questions to Consider:

-   What is the first thing that the initial responders should have done?
-   When making decisions, should the principal have taken the replacement of the chair into consideration?
-   What systems/policies should be implemented to prevent this from happening in the future?

CHAPTER 9

February - March

Chapter 9 includes the following subjects:
- Budget Planning for the Following Year
- Staff Retreat
- Master Schedule for Next Year
- 40-Day Standardized Test Plan
- Planning for Summer School
- Capital Budget Planning Items
- Recruitment Strategy

Much like November, February is a very trying time from a psychological standpoint. Due to daylight savings time, the amount of light that you receive during the month of February is short. If you live in a cold region of the country, that adds to your challenges. During the month of February, it's common for you to report and leave work under the dark skies. Over time, this takes a toll on the principal of the school. In addition to the principal, teachers also experience many of the same challenges. February is a month that needs to be accounted for. Regular words of encouragement from the principal go a long way, especially when staff members are facing adversity.

Another way to motivate teachers during the month of February is to collaboratively plan for the following school year. Through this process, begin to identify future school based leadership and new initiatives for the following year. Allow your staff to become excited and a part of the future of the school. They will appreciate the transparent nature of your actions and support you in moving the school forward.

While the school budget is often monitored and scrutinized throughout the school year, February is a great time to start making budgetary decisions for the following school year. These budgetary decisions could include textbook orders, staffing, furniture, field trips, etc. The vast majority of first year principals inherit the budget design of their predecessors. One of the luxuries of being a principal who will return to the school the following year is the creation of a budget that supports your vision of the school. Creating the school's budget is a thoughtful process. Since you generally have to manage multi-million dollar school budgets, obviously, there is flexibility with the use of the funds. The earlier you start working on the budgetary process for the following year, the more effective you will be as the fiscal manager of the school.

The majority of the school's budget will be devoted to staffing. It is critical to have the most effective staff members in place. By February, you should be well aware of staff members who are ineffective. It is essential that you begin to work them out of their positions. This can be done via conversations, reprimands, emails, etc.; however, you must be clear that their current school is not the place where they should expect to return the following school year. Before making hasty recommendations regarding the non-return of staff, please be aware that collective bargaining agreements (teacher contracts) often require principals to follow specific steps to rid their school of ineffective teachers. Depending on the district/contract, these steps may require an inordinate amount of documentation. If you have a school with a lot of ineffective teachers, you may need to devise a plan to work these teachers out of the building over a period of two years. If the process requires tons of documentation, the principal will need to be selective as to whom he can feasibly dismiss per year. As a first year principal, you do not want to spend your entire first year fighting with ineffective teachers.

Some schools, like many organizations, have staff retreats. As a principal of schools that had retreats and others that did not, I firmly believe that you will need to make the decision regarding the worth of staff retreats. Some of the benefits include the focused discussion around school issues, a chance to relax away from school, the bonding that occurs with staff, and the chance to establish goals. While benefits are worthy, opponents could argue that retreats are too expensive, the topics of discussion are never implemented at school, and the planning time needed for the retreat detracts from the school's current mission. Unfortunately, there is no absolute answer as it relates to retreats. As the principal, you will need to weigh all the pros and cons and proceed accordingly. February is a good month to determine whether the retreat will effectively support your school's mission.

February is a good time to start thinking about the master schedule for the following year. As stated earlier in the book, the master schedule and budget work hand in hand. If you begin thinking about budgetary decisions in February, you must start thinking about your master schedule also. Think about positions, not specific personnel that you would like to see in your school for next year. Your master schedule should dictate whom you need to hire from an instructional standpoint.

March

For a principal, March can be a very stressful month. Most of the stress is rooted in anxiety driven by the statewide standardized test. In the majority of states, this test is administered during the months of March or April. Regardless of how well you have prepared your staff and students for this test, you will undoubtedly be anxious for this period of time to pass.

Principals use a variety of strategies to prepare their students for the standardized test. With sanctions being imposed on schools that do not excel on the test, principals desperately look to gain an advantage in various fashions. Realistically speaking, the schools that generally perform the best on these assessments do minimal preparation specifically focusing on the test. Ironically, schools who fail to excel on standardized tests tend to focus all of their efforts on test preparations. As the principal, you must decide how to attack the test. I have worked in schools (as a teacher) where the school focuses solely on test preparation for a period of 30 days. While I do not agree with this approach, I have a responsibility to share my experiences with you. As a principal, I liked to emphasize both the content and test-taking strategies for a period of 40 school days before the test. I would have teachers incorporate the strategies into their regular instructional plan. This fosters an authentic instructional program through the duration of the testing period.

During the current state of education in which high-stakes testing plays an enormous role, it is easy to over-emphasize the importance of performing on these tests. I strongly discourage any principal from "closing down shop" to solely focus on the preparation of the test. "Closing down shop" describes a situation in which every class in the building, for the entire class period, only focuses on information that pertains to the standardized test. The attempt to solely focus on testing materials and strategies results in severe boredom for students and staff, leading to the underperformance of students on these tests. Incorporate the strategic skills into your teachers' instructional program. It results in a more effective instructional program and supports the academic performance of students.

March is a very challenging month for a variety of reasons. While one may argue that testing is the most critical focal point for the month, the principal must possess the foresight to continue planning for the following year. Your ability to effectively staff the school with high-performing personnel must be a goal. Hiring highly qualified staff members makes your job easier in the long run and supports your students' academic growth. While the task of hiring these staff members may appear to be easy, it actually requires great skill. Hiring average staff is easy; hiring outstanding staff is significantly more challenging. If you have not already done so, begin now to collect resumes and contact potential candidates. The earlier you begin this process, the greater your chances of hiring exceptional staff members. I thoroughly understand that every district conducts its hiring process differently; however, the principal must play an active role in hiring staff, especially teachers. After all staff is hired and the school year is underway, all stakeholders will hold the principal accountable for the quality of education that is being delivered. Principals must not overlook the importance of possessing excellent hiring skills.

* * * * *

SCENARIO

Principals must monitor athletics very closely. From grade changing scandals to ineligible players being permitted to participate, your school's athletic programs have the potential to bring a tremendous amount of negative attention to your school if not monitored.

Every year, students who participate in interscholastic sports have to get a physical examination from a doctor approving their health. Without passing a physical examination, players cannot participate in the sport. Due to the critical nature of physicals as it relates to eligibility, the coach often helps to facilitate the process. For example, to increase the accessibility of a doctor, a coach may arrange to have the doctor conduct physicals at the school. In the district(s) in which I worked, this was common practice. On this occasion, the coach arranged to have a doctor come to the school to conduct the physicals. Approximately three weeks after the physical examinations were completed, I discovered that the person who claimed to be a doctor was actually a physician's assistant who was using the signature of the doctor for whom he worked. This shoddy work by the coach placed our players in harm's way. If a player had sustained a major injury because of being falsely cleared by the physician's assistant, the coach would have definitely lost his teaching/coaching position and I could have possibly lost my position as principal. Fortunately, I discovered the false credentials of the physician's assistant and moved to have an authentic physician conduct the physical examinations on the players. The first game was forfeited due to ineligible players; however, this is nothing when compared to the trouble the school avoided.

Questions to Consider:

- What systems should be implemented to ensure that those who provide services to your students are legitimate?
- If a player sustained a fatal injury as a result of being falsely cleared, who (multiple people) would be held liable for the player's death?
- Due to the potential issues associated with physicals, is it a better practice to totally exclude physicals from being conducted at the school? Why or why not?

CHAPTER 10

April - May

Chapter 10 includes the following subjects:
- Standardized Testing
- Maximizing Spring Break
- Final Evaluations
- Creating a Vision for the Following Year
- Identifying Leaders for the Following Year

For the vast majority of states, April is the month when annual standardized tests are administered. By this time, all staff should be fully aware of the role that they play in administering the test. In April, students, teachers, and parents will be anxious to get the standardized test behind them. As the principal, it is your responsibility to ensure that all issues related to the test are resolved. Even if a testing coordinator has been assigned to complete the tasks associated with these tests, the principal will ultimately be held responsible if the testing does not go well.

One of the challenges associated with April testing is that Spring Break generally comes a few weeks before the testing period. As a principal, you must have a plan to maximize or at least maintain learning opportunities during the Spring Break. Similar to the packets or resources provided to parents over the Winter Break, work must be provided for students over Spring Break. There is a difference between the work provided over Winter Break as compared to Spring Break; the work over Spring Break should have a greater emphasis on skills and content that will be covered on the standardized test. With the great emphasis placed on students' performance on high stakes tests, principals cannot afford to have students miss an entire week of instruction, just a few weeks before the annual test.

Similar to March, principals must have a dual focus during April. While standardized testing is critically important, additional tasks should be completed. For example, principals should plan to finish all teacher observations by the end of April, especially for teachers who are performing in a proficient fashion. Completing their evaluations in April provides the principal with an opportunity to focus professional development on teachers who may have greater challenges during the last few months of the school year. In addition, proficient teachers may be assigned to provide support as mentors for struggling teachers. With the end of the school year quickly approaching, it is in the best interests of the principal to complete the formal evaluation process as early as possible.

With the focus of the entire school placed on testing, it is easy to overlook the planning of the end-of-the-year activities. Graduations, promotional exercises, awards assemblies, etc. require a tremendous amount of planning. These activities often require the ordering of materials (diplomas, trophies, certificates). Due to the high volume of orders submitted at this time of the year, it is important that you allow ample time for your orders to be delivered to the school. April planning should allow enough time for orders to arrive at the school.

The planning for end-of-the-year activities is a perfect opportunity to get your staff to work in committees. I encourage principals to play a limited role on these committees. Of course, the principal needs to play a larger role in the planning of events like graduation; however, events like awards ceremonies could easily be planned by a committee. This provides staff members with a sense of teamwork and lays the foundation for the following year.

April is an ideal time to begin to plan for the summer. By this time of year, fatigue will begin to set in; however, you must realize the summer is just around the corner. Even though the vast majority of summer work is completed in July, your ability to effectively plan for the work must begin much earlier. This is especially important for projects that require more than the typical length of summer (two months) to complete. For these projects, you may want to start much sooner. For example, minor building renovations, setting up portable classrooms, redesigning classroom spaces, etc. are projects that may require an extended period of time to complete. The key to finishing these projects before the opening of school is to start planning and executing early.

May

Even though earlier chapters have suggested that you begin focusing on the ensuing school year, May is the month for the final "warning shot." Unfortunately, by May, your current school year is over. Any policies that you failed to implement will not be implemented between May and the end of the school year. As a principal, May is the month that you determine the trajectory of the school for the following academic year. More importantly, May is the month that you decide on the steps required to achieve the goals for the following school year.

To begin the planning process for the following year, you must conduct a serious review of policies that you want to implement in the upcoming school year. To maximize the level of buy-in from your staff, include staff members in the analysis of last year's policies and the creation of next year's policies. School uniform policies, meeting protocols, student registration procedures all need to be examined. Of course, the procedures specific to your school will differ from what I suggested. At any rate, examine the policies that you have in place with the goal of planning for next year.

May will prove to be a critical month. Like principals, teachers need to plan for the following school year. If you have evaluated teachers and other staff members throughout the school year, you are fully aware of the assignment changes that need to be made for the following year. You must have a diversity of approaches when requesting changes in teacher assignments.   In obvious cases, every person in the school knows the change in a teacher's assignment that needs to be made. In general, these requests usually go uncontested by the teacher. On the other hand, some requests will be very difficult. Teachers will provide every reason why the change will not benefit the school. To contest this, always have a few reasons why the change is needed. As a principal, remain firm in your decision. Remember that your word is final, so act accordingly. When your word is final, you must lay the groundwork for the finality of your decision. Do not abuse your power.

If you ask any teacher, they are more than willing to share stories about their favorite and worst class. Obviously, classes are based on individual students. The composition of students that make up a class is of critical importance. As a principal, you will not have the depth of knowledge required to create an effective class list. Even if you base class lists on indicators like standardized test results or report card grades, there are so many additional factors that contribute to the welfare of a class. No one in the school knows a student better than a teacher. Allow teachers to create class lists for the following year. As a school, you will need to determine whether you want heterogeneous or homogeneous classes, but teachers should complete the actual placing of students. Therefore, the current fourth grade teachers should be creating the class lists of next year's fifth grade classes. If done in May, parents are provided enough time for feedback and teachers can prepare for the following school year.

As a new principal, selecting team leaders for the past year may have been a challenging process. Because you have been a principal for almost a complete school year, this process should be much easier.

Throughout the year, teacher leaders became apparent. These are the teachers who always volunteered to lead a committee or worked with the struggling teacher. Staff members throughout the school respected their leadership characteristics. In May, the principal should identify these school leaders for the following school year. This process should be transparent, but the final decision should be that of the principal.

*   *   *   *   *

SCENARIO

As a principal, your role of instructional leader will be overshadowed by the many roles that you will be forced to play because of your position. On this spring morning, I sat in the congregation of a funeral for an active parent who died suddenly. His two elementary-aged children were a product of a difficult union of two adults. The father was a recovering drug addict while the mother was already deceased from HIV. Close relatives were fighting over the guardianship of the children, not because they cared about their well being, but rather to gain control of the money that was due to the children. As I sat in the funeral, I knew that relatives were going to attempt to use the school to gain leverage over the guardianship battle. In my usual way, I snuck into the rear of the funeral home and sat in the third from the last pew. My goal was to go unnoticed; however, when my students saw me, they called my name, blowing my cover. Immediately after the service, adults began to introduce themselves to me, all of them saying they would come to see me during the following week. My experience told me to remain distant. I simply did not want to involve the school in family relations. While I admired the family for pulling the funeral together, I was determined not to have the school participate in determining the custody of the children. I loved the children; however, the court system would need to determine the guardianship, without the help of the school.

Questions to Consider

- Knowing the family members had personal agendas, should the principal have attended the funeral?
- Does the school have a responsibility to make suggestions as to who should be the guardian?
- In the absence of the mother or father, is it acceptable for the students to reside with a teacher from the school until guardianship is resolved.

CHAPTER 11

June

Chapter 11 includes the following subjects:
- Plan for "Closing" the School
- Professional Development for Teachers
- Effective use of Teachers

In the vast majority of states, June marks the end of the school year. As a principal, you are looking forward to the end of the year probably more than students. The summer will result in a small amount of relaxation, but remember, the work of the principal never really ends. Enjoy June, because the work cycle will resume very quickly in July.

One thing that you need to realize is that teachers will no longer be present after the last day of school. As you know, 10-month employees play a critical role in the operation of the school. Any tasks that need to be completed before teachers leave for the summer must be completed by the last day of school. I know this advice may seem like common sense; however, when you report to work after the last day of school, you will realize how little support you have with the exception of office support. For example, if the fire marshal conducts an inspection of the school during the summer months and discovers that the conditions within teachers' closets have fire code violations, then it will be the principal's responsibility to resolve this situation without the support of teachers. Maximize the use of your teachers before they leave for the summer. While some teachers are willing to attend meetings over the summer, others will be inaccessible.

The task of effectively preparing the school for the summer months can be overwhelming. The goal of this process is to store all items to ensure a smooth unpacking upon the teachers' return in August. To achieve this, collaborate with all in-house stakeholders to determine what needs to be accounted for. For example, the media specialist may serve as the point person for teachers to submit their laptop computers, whereas the book clerk may be responsible for accepting and storing all teachers' manuals (textbooks). A checklist can be created that lists the person who is responsible for each specific area. Require each key person to provide a signature for teachers who satisfy the submission of articles for that area. The checkout phase will occur over a period of weeks. Suggested areas that should be addressed for the appropriate closing of school are as follows: textbook collection, grade submission, completion of cumulative files, securing of computers, bulletin board removal, locker clean up, etc. Of course the items needed for your school's appropriate closing will be specific for your school.

For the principal, the goal of June is to make it to the last day of school for teachers and students. By this point, all that has happened throughout the school year is history. Any major problems that you encountered during the year can be corrected over the summer months. Because of all the activities associated with the end of the year, June is a hectic month. The end-of -year staff evaluations, closing of classrooms, storing of supplies, and securing of technology all take an enormous amount of planning and are time consuming to execute. Undoubtedly, the pressure that builds because of end-of-the-year activities will cease on the final day of the school year.

The last day of school is an enjoyable time for all staff. To celebrate the day, you may want to provide an ice cream social or lunch. This is the perfect opportunity to present certificates of appreciation or a small token for their support throughout the school year. For teachers who are not returning, the last day of school will mark the final time that they will be in the building. Remember, you and your staff have just completed a momentous journey--treat it accordingly.

In some schools, professional development days are required at the end of the school year. As the leader of the school, you will need to decide how to best utilize these days. Time devoted to professional development right before a two-month summer break is usually not time well spent. It may be a good time to give a preview of changes that are set to occur for the next school year, but other than that, you will need to decide on how you want to proceed.

*   *   *   *   *

SCENARIO

Strange things tend to happen near the end of the school year. For this reason, it is critical to have a comprehensive plan in place for successfully making it through the school days.

During dismissal time, on a warm June afternoon, in the front of the school, a dog bit a student. As the boy screamed in pain, security guards rushed to the scene. Luckily, one of our teachers had worked previously as an EMT. He was immediately summoned to the scene to provide medical treatment. He applied a tourniquet to the student's leg. While the student was being treated, an emergency 911 call was placed. Before school officials could contact the parent, a student who witnessed the incident ran to the mother's house and informed her of the event. Within seconds of each other, the mother and medics arrived at the scene. While some students' parents remain calm during stressful situations, his mother did not fall into this category. She was very uncooperative and unruly. She was upset about the incident and was even more upset about not being contacted by an administrator. To complicate matters, she did not want her child transported to the hospital. So any hope of her leaving the scene to accompany her child to the hospital was lost. I finally gained control over the situation by promising to meet with her in the presence of a police officer the next morning. In the event that she wanted to file criminal charges, I chose to include the police officer in the conference. During the meeting, the mother claimed that she knew the girl who was responsible for ordering the dog to bite her son. She stated that the act was in retaliation for her child's dog biting the girl a few days earlier. Hearing this information, the police officer asked if she wanted to press charges against the girl; however, the parent refused. Approximately one month later, I received a call from the parent's attorney stating that they wanted to file a lawsuit against the school for failing to create a safe environment for students at dismissal time.

Questions to Consider

- Can the school/school district be held liable for a dog biting a student on school grounds?
- Should the parent have been contacted before the medics?
- After being informed of the pending lawsuit, what documentation should be collected to support the decisions of the principal?

Conclusion

Your first year of principalship is the hardest. Like the first year as a teacher, all stakeholders will once again try to determine who you are as a leader and as a person. Undoubtedly, subsequent years should get progressively easier. If you are able to remain in your school, your battles will change or evolve over time. As you lead your organization, you will surely identify areas that were non-factors during year one. I compare the difference between your first and second year as a principal to the difference between your freshman and sophomore year in college. As a freshman, you typically knew very little about campus, students, professors, or courses; however, as a sophomore, you had your entire year planned before you returned to school in the fall. As a principal, year two should be drastically easier than year one.

As you plan to embark on your second year as a school leader, remember the mistakes that you made during your first year. While it may have started poorly, you now have a golden opportunity to address all of those first-year shortcomings that you experienced. Even though you are ecstatic regarding the conclusion of your first school year, take time to reflect about last year's journey. This will be your only way to effectively plan for the future.

Once you have successfully completed your first year, you have the responsibility to support others who succeed you. As an experienced principal, you possess a wealth of knowledge that will be beneficial to first year principals. As a life-long educator, you should not only continue to learn, but should continue to teach. Accept the responsibility to support new principals. Even in cases where the competitive nature between schools does not lend itself to the sharing of best practices, your interests should lie in developing outstanding leadership in all schools. Ultimately, this strengthens our educational system, maximizing the academic potential in both students and teachers. As a principal, you continue to benefit from the same education system that helped to develop your own skills. Hold yourself accountable to ensure our school systems continue to function. Principals, you are the key.

Appendix

[Letterhead]

July 10, 2010

Dear Parent(s):

I am eagerly looking forward to providing your child with the finest education that the Trenton City Public Schools has to offer. Because your child's teenage years are so critical, I understand the importance of selecting the best junior high school. With the goal of developing well-rounded students, we have created a nurturing environment, allowing our students to thrive.

The teachers at Franklin have committed themselves to delivering a rigorous instructional program. To challenge our students, we have a Gifted and Talented Program. In addition, our students thoroughly enjoy our Humanities Program. Through these programs, our students take advanced courses including Spanish I, Spanish II, Algebra I, Algebra II, Geometry, Environmental Science, Biology, and Honors English. We believe our academic program is comparable to that of any school across the city. I know your child will be an asset to our fine academic program.

The Franklin JHS family prides itself on meeting the needs of all its students. With a wide variety of programs offered during and after school, your child will always be engaged in activities that promote academic and social growth. Furthermore, Franklin JHS participates in

TCIAA interscholastic athletic programs. Our sports teams include football, basketball, cheerleading, softball, baseball, track and field, and volleyball. We are extremely proud of our student-athletes and are always looking for new members to join our teams. Through an outstanding partnership with the Trenton/Hopewell Family Support Collaborative (THFSC), we provide services for the entire family. THFSC offers parenting workshops, mentoring programs, home-buying seminars, college saving seminars, and more. I have included a pamphlet and a school newsletter highlighting many of the activities we offer.

We have an "open door" policy, and I invite you to visit us at Franklin JHS. If you have any questions, do not hesitate to contact me at 202-XXX-XXXX. I look forward to working with you to achieve your child's educational goals.

Sincerely,

Keith T. Stephenson
Principal

Encls: Pamphlet and newsletter

Welcome Letter to New Teacher

[Letterhead]

June 30, 2010

Dear Judy Jackson:

I would like to welcome you to the Franklin JHS family. I am extremely pleased to have the opportunity to develop a professional relationship with you. As a new member of our teaching staff, I am eagerly looking forward to introducing you to your new colleagues. We truly believe in the team concept and want to embrace you as our newest star player. Together, we will work tirelessly to provide the finest instructional program to our students.

Even though I have officially offered you a position at Franklin, the process will not be complete until your documentation has been submitted and approved by the Human Resource Department. To expedite the process, please complete the employment application, provide two letters of recommendation, and have a TB (tuberculosis) test conducted by your physician. Take these documents to Human Resources when you report. Franklin JHS has submitted the appropriate documentation to begin your hiring process so you should be hearing from Human Resources in the next few weeks. If you have questions about this process, do not hesitate to contact me. Again, welcome aboard.

Sincerely,

Keith T. Stephenson
Principal

Welcome Letter to Teachers

[Letterhead]

July 27, 2010

Dear Rutherford Staff Member:

Throughout the summer, the staff has been working to ensure that Rutherford gets off to a great start. Our staff will consist of over 80 staff members. Regardless of your role or job description at Rutherford, you play an important role in the academic and social development of our students. At this point, we only have one vacancy and I hope it will be filled within the next week. Every new staff member comes with a variety of unique experiences that will surely strengthen our school.

We made AYP in mathematics but failed to make AYP in reading. In reading, our schoolwide score exceeded the academic target; however, based on NCLB, all subgroups must also meet their academic targets. In our special education subgroup, we actually missed our AYP target in reading by 1.5 students. While our work last year demonstrated the progress that we have made as a staff, our challenge is to maximize the academic achievements of all our students. Based on higher academic targets, our academic goals must be increased. As a newly-formed staff, we possess the ability to have 100% of our students score proficient on next year's standardized test.

Thank you for your commitment to our students and I look forward to developing a professional relationship with you. I have attached a list of critical dates for the start of the school year. Please adhere to the schedule. If you have questions, do not hesitate to contact me. Enjoy the remainder of your summer and prepare yourself for greatness.

Educationally yours,

Keith Stephenson
Principal

Welcome Letter to Teachers

[Letterhead]

July 24, 2010

Dear Sussex MS Staff Member:

Throughout the summer, the staff has been working to ensure that Sussex MS has its finest year in our school's extensive history. We will be welcoming six new teachers to our staff. Additionally, we will have a resident principal through the "New Leaders for Urban Schools" program, serving the role of an assistant principal. They all come with a variety of experiences that will surely strengthen our instructional program.

Even though we made great strides last school year, it is time to refocus our efforts on becoming the best middle school in the city. To attract and retain the top students, we must offer a rigorous instructional program that challenges each one of our students. Additionally, we must work collaboratively to plan creative lessons, design new strategies, and implement new ideas. I am overcome by excitement when I think of our collective potential. I know we have the best staff in the county; however, we must work to prove this by developing and publicizing our impressive work through our students.

For teachers, school starts on August 22, 2010 at 8:00 a.m. As always, I will conduct a "Welcome Back" meeting and provide time to prepare your classroom. Due to the physical work that must be completed during the first week, please feel free to dress casually. The first day of school for students will be August 28, 2010. If you have any questions do not hesitate to contact me. Welcome Back!

Educationally yours,

Keith Stephenson
Principal

Back To School Night Memorandum

To: All Teachers

From: Keith Stephenson

Date: 9/18/10

Re: Back to School Night

As you know, Back to School Night will be held this Wednesday from 6:00-8:00. Attached is the schedule. Promptly at 6:00, our program will begin in the auditorium. In order to be introduced, all teachers should be present . At approximately 6:25, all parents will be dismissed to their child's homeroom class to follow their child's schedule. Students' schedules will be distributed at the front door. The Back to School Night schedule is as follows.

HR 6:30-6:35
Pd 1 6:38-6:48
Pd 26:51-7:10
Pd 37:03-7:12
Pd 47:15-7:24
Pd 57:27-7:36
Pd 67:39-7:48
Pd 77:51-8:00

Back to School Night Suggestions

Classroom Setup
- Make sure all bulletin boards are complete
- Have desks neatly arranged
- Remove all derogatory and profane language from desks and walls
- Have students' work posted throughout room
- De-clutter teacher's desk and classroom

Talking Points

- Discuss expectations and class routines
- Discuss syllabus, homework, and major (yearly) projects
- Explain ways to get an "A" in your class

Handouts
- Be prepared to hand out syllabus
- Class material list

Suggestions
- Know all of your students' names
- Have students' grades available
- Keep conversations short. Set up conferences for later dates (with entire team if needed).
- Be Positive. Speak highly of (school name) and (school district).
- Remember, you represent (school name).
- Give parents directions to next class.
- Be Brief. Periods are only 9 minutes long.

Form for Collecting Data on Staff Members

[School Name]

[Administrators' Names]

DATA COLLECTION FORM
SY 2009-2010

Name of Employee: _____

Date	Documented Performance	Comments
	Non-Compliance With Duty Schedule	
	Failure to Perform Hall Duty	
	Parent Complaints	
	Student Complaints	
	Tardy to Class	
	Tardy to Coverage Assignments	
	Timely Submission of Reports	
	Readiness for Students	
	Excessive Disciplinary Referrals	
	Excluding Students from Class	
	Leaving Students Unsupervised	
	Failure to Post Student Grades	
	Unexcused Absence (Teacher/Faculty Meeting)	
	Failure to Change Bulletin Board	
	Failure to Initiate/Follow-up Parental Contact	
	Failure to Provide Lesson Plans	
	Failure to submit attendance	
	Late to Work	
	Other:	
	Other:	

Administrator: _____ Date: _____

cc: Note to File

Informal Observation Checklist

Teacher: _____

_____ **Classroom Aesthetics**
- current student work posted
- bulletin boards current and complete
- desks free of graffiti
- data walls

_____ **Chalkboard**
- daily agenda
- objective
- homework
- standard

Rubric
3- Highly Visible
2- Somewhat Visible
1- Signs of Visibility
0- Non-Existent

_____ **Level of Rigor of Instruction**
- worksheet or authentic work
- high level of student engagement
- students' heads on desk
- accurate assessments being conducted

_____ **Teacher Behaviors**
- - Teacher seated or standing
- - Teacher actively engaged in delivering instruction
- - Teacher actively monitoring student work
- - Teacher actively assessing student knowledge

Lesson Plans available on desk (hard copy)?   Yes   No

Additional Comments:
_____
_____
_____
_____
_____
_____

Administrator: _____ Date: _____

cc: Note to File

Standardized Classroom Checklist

Jane Doe Campus

Teacher: _____**Date:** _____

Student Work

_____ Current Work (within 1 month)
_____ Publishable Quality
_____ Constructive Feedback
_____ Standardized Heading (including date)
_____ Everything present. Great Job!!!

Data Walls

_____ Current Literacy Benchmark Data (Head Start-Grade 2 only)
_____ Current Standardized Test Data (Grades 3-8 only)
_____ Student codes posted with the data
_____ Everything present. Great Job!!!

Comments:

_____
_____
_____
_____
_____
_____
_____

Administrator: _____ Date: _____

cc: Note to File

Administrative Responsibilities

The Jane Doe Academy
SY 2009-2010

K. Stephenson	T. Foster	M. Harbor	V. King
PK-8 Grade Students	PS-4 Grade Students (Lower School)	5th -8th Grade Students (Upper School)	PS-8th Grade Students Behavior Management Program
Lunch Duty (gr. 3-5)	Lower School Parent Club	Upper School Parent Club	PK-8th Student Incentive Program (3)
Professional Development	Coordinate lunch (PS-K)	Lunch (6-8)	Breakfast Duty
Safety and Security	Lunch Duty (gr. 1-2)	Substitute Coverage Upper School	Track and Report Behavior Date or Data?(Student/Teacher) (1st and 15th/month)
Facility Issues	Substitute Coverage Lower School	Performance Management Implementation	Community Partnerships
Special education	Implementation of Local School Plan	Implementation of Local School Plan	Attend grade? level meetings
Clerical Staff	Teacher Appreciation Week	Teacher Appreciation Week	Student Leadership Committee
All Assessments	Academic Recognition Ceremony Coordinator (lower school)	Academic Recognition Ceremony Coordinator (upper school)	Coordinate the in school suspension program
Staffing	Performance Management Implementation		Lunch (6-8)

Administrative Responsibilities (Cont'd)

K. Stephenson	T. Foster	M. Harbor	V. King
Budget	Professional Development	Professional Development	AM/PM Duty
Oversight of All Duties	Guidance/Support Staff Dept.	New Teacher Academy	
New Teacher Academy	All assessments	Educational Aides	
AM/PM Duty	New Teacher Academy	Fire Drills	
	Teacher Appreciation Week	Substitute/Class Coverage (PK-8)	
	AM/PM Duty	Teacher Appreciation Week	
		All assessments	
		AM/PM Duty	

Summer Schedule

Task	Responsible Person	Date to Be Complete	Percent Complete	Completed
Registration	Williams	Ongoing		
Registration Packet (to go home with parents upon registration)	Myers			
Student Handbook	Stephenson, Foster, Harbor	July 24		
Copies of Student Handbook	Myers	August 1		
Write Welcome Letter To Teachers	Stephenson	July 15		
Mail Welcome Letters to Teachers	Williams	July 17		
Compile Teacher Email Addresses (JPCS and personal)	Williams	July 24		
Staffing Update	Stephenson	Ongoing		
Textbook/material Inventory	Miner	July 22		
Create instructional material list for each grade level	Instructional Coaches	July 22		
Order Textbooks/supplies	Miner	July 24		
Schoolwide Discipline Plan (Pre K- 4, 5-8)	King, admin team, teachers	July 31		
Create at least 3 Behavior Incentive Plans	King	July 24		
Copies of Schoolwide Discipline Plan Completed	Williams	July 31		
Classroom Assignments	Foster/ Stephenson	July 17		
Office Assignments	Stephenson and admin team	July 17		
Call Perspective Parents to Register (Create log)	Browning	Ongoing		
Develop/define Counselor roles	Foster, Chris	July 24		

Summer Schedule (cont'd)

Develop Logistical Plan (entry, exit, lunch, class passing, disciplinary issues)	Stephenson and admin team	July 31		
Redo Documents (Conference letter, coverage slip, any doc with Brown JHS on it)	Williams	July 31		
Order Hallpasses (slips for counselors, office, etc)	Miner	July 17		
Order pails and baskets (hall passes)	Miner	July 17		
Reorganize Filing System (101 and Main Office) Throw away old and create current year file	Custodial Staff	July 10		
All storage closets cleaned and trash discarded	Cutodial Staff, Foster, Harbour, King	July 17		
Print Student Schedules	Brown	August 1		
Print Master Schedules	Brown	August 1		
Sp. Ed Inclusion Plan	Waters/ Teachers/Foster	July 17		
Create Class Lists	Harbour/ Teachers	July 17		
Create "Specials" schedule	Foster	July 17		
Create Calendar Template	Harbour	June 24		
Order Supplies	Miner	Ongoing		
Update Evacuation Plan	Miner	July 31		
Copies of Evacuation Plan	Miner	August 14		
Plan for Back to School Activities (ex. Teacher Handbooks)	Foster/ Stephenson/ Teachers	July 31		
Personnel Action Forms/Contracts	Miner	Ongoing		
Attend Monday Meetings	All Staff	Ongoing		
Create Paraprofessional Schedules	Foster	August 7		
Business Cards	Miner	August 7		
Order 5 printers	Miner	ASAP		
Coordinate Furniture Move	Harbour	August 3-7		

SAMPLE BULLETIN

GEAR CAMPUS

March 1-6, 2010

Thought for the Week
Children may forget what you say, but they'll
never forget how you make them feel.
~ Palmer

Special Thanks To:
- Mr. Hines for providing sound support for all of our programs last week. It would not have worked without you.
- Ms. Willard and Ms. McDell for coordinating the PLC's. Great Job.
- Ms. Brown for serving as the coordinator of the Open House last week. Job well done.

1. ACTIVITIES FOR THIS WEEK:
- *Monday* -Counselor's mtg. (9:00)
- *Tuesday* –Achievement Block (3:30-4:15, ELA)
- *Wednesday* –New Teacher's Mtg. with Ms. Abbott Davis (3:30)
- Data Talks
- *Thursday*-Achievement Block (3:30-4:15, Math)
- *Friday* – Police Band Assembly 1:30-3:00 (select classes only)
- Saturday-Saturday School (Our attendance goal is 100 students)

2. **Data Talks:** Data talks are on Thursday during planning periods

3. **Attention Teachers:** STUDENTS ARE NOT TO BE EXCLUDED BECAUSE THEY LACK SUPPLIES OR THEY ARE TARDY.

4. **Reminder: Important March Dates:**

    9th – PAC Mtg. (6:00 PM)
    15th- Leadership Presentation for Chairman of the Board
    19th- No School for Students (Professional Development Day)
    26th- Early Release Day (12:15 dismissal)
    29th- Start of Spring Break (3.29-4.5)

5. **Students with F's:** Teachers are responsible for communicating low grades to parents ASAP. Do not wait until mid advisory reports or conference days. Contact parents as soon as students' grades begin to drop.

6. **REQUESTING LEAVE.** When you know you need to request leave (sick, emergency, etc.), please call Ms. Foster or Mr. Harbour directly. Do not use your colleagues to call for you.

7. **The Chamberlain Way-** Let's do everything right every day. It will only be successful if you support the system.

8. **REMINDER:** Upper school teachers are expected to actively perform hall duty between each period and before and after school.

9. **Lunch time procedures**: All teachers must escort students quietly to the cafeteria. Teachers of grades 1-5 should retrieve students from the playground with five minutes remaining in the period.

10. **Attention Teachers**: Students should walk on the right side of the hall at all times. Active hall supervision will support the implementation of this rule...the Gold Standard.

11. **Videos/Movies:** Movies are not to be shown in class unless approved by an administrator. Movies must be connected to class content and not simply used to fill time. Approval must be requested at least two days in advance.

12. **Hall Pass System.** Students should never be released from your class without a pass. Please use the basket pass. If you have any questions/concerns, ask Mr. Stephenson. Let's all continue to work to make it a success.

13. **Bulletin Announcements.** Announcements for next week's bulletin should be submitted to Ms. Williamson by the close of business Wednesday.

14. **Observations.** Informal observations will be conducted regularly.

15. **Recess:** Please feel free to use the both the gym and alley side door to return from recess. Be sure students are quiet when they enter the main hallway.

Pointless Fact of the Week
If you doubled one penny every day for 30 days,
you would have $5,368,709.12.

END OF THE YEAR TEACHER CLEARANCE FORM

*Name*_____

The following is a checklist for teachers to complete by the close of school on **Tuesday, June 22, 2010**. Please secure the designated signature for each item. The completed checklist should be submitted to Dr. Stephenson. Please do not leave your clearance sheet with the office staff.

Completing the clearance process is one of your professional responsibilities. Failure to submit the clearance checklist will result in a written addendum to your final rating form. Your cooperation is appreciated.

Checklist Item Signature of Certifier

1. **LAPTOP RETURN/ AV EQUIPMENT** _____

   Mr. Mathews

2. **CONDITION OF INSTRUCTIONAL AREA** _____

   Clean classroom   Mr. Harbour/Ms. Foster

3. **FURNITURE REPAIR REQUEST** _____

   Contact person and equipment location .   Mr. Herns

4. **FINAL GRADES** _____

   entered into POWERSCHOOL   Ms. Brown

5. **FINANCIAL REPORTS** _____

   Ms. Mills

6. **SUMMER ADDRESS CARD** _____
   (Each Staff Member must Complete a Card)   Ms. Williams/
                                                            Ms. Elton

7. **TEXTBOOK REPORT** _____
   Any textbook requests should be made to   Ms. Willis
   Ms. Miller via instructional coach.

8. **LOCKER CLEARANCE** _____
   (Homeroom Teachers)Mr. King

9. **ANNUAL EVALUATION** _____
   (All ratings must be signed by Tuesday,   Dr. Stephenson
   June 22, 2010 without exception)

10. **KEYS-ALL IN UNSEALED ENVELOPES** _____
    (Elevator, Classroom, etc.)   Ms. Williams

11. **IEP'S** _____
    (Special Education Teachers only)   Ms. Watson

12. **FINAL CLEARANCE CHECKLIST** _____
    (Submit to Dr. Stephenson   Dr. Stephenson
    by Tuesday, 6/22/10)

END OF YEAR STUDENT CLOSEOUT FORM

BALDWIN JUNIOR HIGH SCHOOL

Check Out Sheet
(9th Grade)

Name: _____ School Year _____ Section _____

Teachers, please do not sign unless the student is debt free and has fulfilled all obligations.

Period	Subject	Materials to be Returned	Teacher's Signature

Textbooks _____   Locks _____   Sports Uniforms _____
          Ms. Merritt/Mr. Till   HR Teacher   Ms. Welsh

Portfolio _____   9th Grade Class Debts _____
          Ms. Perry

This is to certify that the above-named student has cleared his/her record.

Section Teacher _____ **Counselor** _____

Asst. Principal _____ **Principal** _____

INVITATIONS RECEIVED _____

Students must receive signatures from teachers during the time they are assigned to them. Students will be informed as to when they are to acquire the signatures of all other staff members.

Sample School Closing Flyers

February 9, 2010, Professional Development Day

Franklin Middle School will close at 12:00pm on Wednesday, February 9, 2010, for Professional Development Day.

School will reopen on Thursday, February 10, 2010, at the regular time.

Sincerely,

Dr. Keith Stephenson
Principal
Franklin Middle School

Washington Elementary School Closings

Chamberlain Elementary School will be closed on
Monday, January 19, 2009, in observance of
Martin Luther King's birthday.

Chamberlain Elementary School will be
closed on Tuesday, January 20, 2009,
for the Presidential Inauguration.

School will reopen on Wednesday, January 21, 2009.

Sample Interview Questions for Teacher Candidates

1. Aside from your resume, is there anything else you would like to share with the panel?
2. What is you philosophy of education?
3. What should a person expect to see when entering your classroom during an instructional period?
4. Describe the perfect lesson
5. Can you name the essential components of a lesson and explain their importance in the instructional process?
6. How do you accommodate for varying learning styles in your classroom?
7. Can you describe a data-driven instructional program?
8. How do you incorporate data into your instructional practices?
9. What types of classroom routines do you establish to ensure a smooth instructional period/day?
10. Do you understand the effects of poverty on students' educational process? Please explain
11. Scenario- You have a student repeatedly disturbing your class by calling out, what steps would you take to curb this behavior?
12. Aside from teaching, in what other capacity would you be willing to serve at Baxter Middle School?
13. What would you describe as your strengths and weaknesses?
14. Do you have questions for the panel?

Sample Interview Questions for Asst. Principal Candidates

1. Aside from your resume, is there anything else you would like to share with the panel?
2. What do you think it takes to be successful as an Assistant Principal?
3. Explain what you would do your first month at a school.
4. When evaluating a teacher, what indicators do you think are critical in determining their level of performance?
5. What does an effective classroom look like?
6. Explain how Regular Education and Special Education teachers can work together to help all students be successful.
7. You will be supervising the custodial staff. What steps will you take to establish credibility with this group of employees?
8. Give me an example of how you resolved a student discipline problem.
9. How would you approach a situation when a student is sent to the office for discipline issues? How would you handle "repeat offenders."
10. What are your feelings about the No Child Left Behind Act and AYP (Annual Yearly Progress)?
11. How often should staff members expect to see you around the school, in classrooms, etc.?
12. How would you help a struggling teacher?
13. How would you describe yourself in terms of your ability to work as a   member of a team?
14. We can sometimes identify a small problem and fix it before it becomes a major problem. Give an example(s) of how you have done this.
15. Describe a time when you had to deal with an upset parent.
16. What kind of supervisor do you work best for? Provide examples.

17. In your opinion, explain which of the five senses is most crucial to developing interpersonal relationships with staff?

18. How would you like the teachers in our school to describe you as an assistant principal?

19. Why should we hire you?

20. Do you have any additional questions for the panel?

SAMPLE MASTER SCHEDULE

Monument Master Schedule (2010-2011)

Class	HR 8:00-8:20	Pd 1 8:20-9:02	Pd 2 9:06- 9:48	Pd 3 9:52-10:34
Pre k3 (Brown)	HR/MM	Reading	Reading	Writer's Workshop
(Suess)	HR/MM	Reading	Reading	Writer's Workshop
Pre K4 (Jackson)	HR/MM	Reading	Reading	Writer's Workshop
(Ruddick)	HR/MM	Reading	Reading	Writer's Workshop
(Lasko)	HR/MM	Reading	Reading	Writer's Workshop
Kinder-garden (Basso)	HR/MM	Reading	Reading	Writer's Workshop
(Lester)	HR/MM	Reading	Reading	Writer's Workshop
(Mia)	HR/MM	Reading	Reading	Writer's Workshop
Grade 1 (Smith)	HR/MM	Reading	Reading	Specials
(Byrd)	HR/MM	Reading	Reading	Specials
(Jackson)	HR/MM	Reading	Reading	Specials
Grade 2 (Harbor)	HR/MM	Reading	Reading	Specials
(Branch)	HR/MM	Reading	Reading	Specials
(Price)	HR/MM	Reading	Reading	Specials
Grade 3 (Joyce)	HR/MM	Reading	Reading	SS/Science
(Bush)	HR/MM	Reading	Reading	SS/Science
(Gaines)	HR/MM	Reading	Reading	Writer's Workshop

Monument Master Schedule (2010-2011)

Pd4 10:38-11:20	Pd 5 11:24-12:06	Pd 6 12:10-12:52	Pd 7 12:56-1:40	Pd 8 1:44-2:26	Pd 9 2:30-3:12
SS/Science	Lunch/ Recess	NAP	Specials	Math	Math
SS/Science	Lunch/ Recess	NAP	Specials	Math	Math
Specials	Lunch/ Recess (classroom)	NAP	Math	Math	SS/Science
Specials	Lunch/ Recess (classroom)	NAP	Math	Math	SS/Science
Specials	Lunch/ Recess (classroom)	NAP	Math	Math	SS/Science
Specials	Recess/ Lunch	Math	Math	SS/Science	SS/Science
Specials	Recess/ Lunch	Math	Math	SS/Science	SS/Science
Specials	Recess/ Lunch	Math	Math	SS/Science	SS/Science
Writer's Workshop	Recess/ Lunch	Math	Math	ss/science	ss/science
Writer's Workshop	Recess/ Lunch	Math	Math	ss/science	ss/science
Writer's Workshop	Recess/ Lunch	Math	Math	ss/science	ss/science
Writer's Workshop	Recess/ Lunch	Math	Math	ss/science	ss/science
Writer's Workshop	Recess/ Lunch	Math	Math	ss/science	ss/science
Writer's Workshop	Recess/ Lunch	Math	Math	ss/science	ss/science
SS/Science	Lunch/ Recess	Writer's Workshop	Specials	Math	Math
SS/Science	Lunch/ Recess	Writer's Workshop	Specials	Math	Math
SS/Science	SS/Science	Lunch/ Recess	Specials	Math	Math

* All classes from 4th-8th grade are departmentalized.

About the Author

 Dr. Keith Stephenson has dedicated his life to working with students in urban schools. His teaching career began as an elementary school teacher in Trenton, NJ. Pursuing an administrative position, Dr. Stephenson began working with the District of Columbia Schools (DCPS). During his tenure with DCPS, he served as a teacher, assistant principal, and principal. While some people frown upon the notion of working in urban schools, Dr. Stephenson is driven by the challenge of changing the lives of both students and their families.

Currently, Dr. Stephenson serves as the principal of the Friendship Public Charter School, Chamberlain Campus, located in Washington, DC. In his former principalship within DCPS, Dr. Stephenson led a multimillion dollar renovation and transformation of a traditional junior high school into an educational campus, a school serving grades prekindergarten through eighth. Under his leadership in multiple schools, suspension rates decreased by over 60%, the number of honor roll students increased by 40%, and truancy rates decrease by over 40%. Dr. Stephenson has a masterful understanding of the systems needed to transform difficult school cultures into high functioning learning environments. In all schools where Dr. Stephenson works, he understands the importance of addressing the various needs of the "whole child" through education.

Keith Stephenson received his undergraduate degree from Lehigh University, Masters Degree from Bowie State University, and Doctorate Degree from The George Washington University. Through all of his educational endeavors, he remains committed to developing communities by effectively educating their citizens.

Keith Stephenson was born and raised in Willingboro, NJ. He currently resides in Washington, DC with his wife, Jameca, and three sons, Bryce, Justin, and Grant.

Please feel free to contact Dr. Stephenson
at kts318@yahoo.com.

CPSIA information can be obtained at www.ICGtesting.com
Printed in the USA
LVOW051948060912

297702LV00008B/82/P